My Scotland is a book of fragments, an attempt to catch and probe what it means to be Scottish. The author has lived, as he once termed it, 'abroad' for the last thirty-eight 58 years, and now looks back at the dark springs and origins of his own obsessions. This is a personal view of Scotland, not a travelogue, or a history: the short prose passages make up a broken landscape, a country of the mind; perhaps, as George Macbeth once called it himself in an early poem, 'the dream-Scotland grief was noble in'.

MY SCOTLAND

fragments of a state of mind

MY SCOTLAND

fragments of a state of mind

George MacBeth

Macmillan

SBN Boards: 333 14134 2

Published by Macmillan London Limited
London and Basingstoke
Associated companies in New York Dublin
Melbourne Johannesburg and Madras

Printed in Great Britain by
REDWOOD PRESS LIMITED
Trowbridge, Wiltshire

FOREWORD

This book is perhaps the nearest I shall come to writing an autobiography. For the record, I was born in Shotts, Lanarkshire, in 1932, moved with my parents to Billingham, then Sheffield, when I was four, was educated there, returned to Hamilton and Dundee regularly for holidays. My father worked in a mine when I was born, became a colliery engineer and draughtsman, died in the uniform of an officer of the Home Guard during an air-raid in 1941. My mother died of a liver disease when I was 19, and still at school. These facts are at the root of this book. It was composed in short bursts, rarely more than about six sections a day, between August 1969 and September 1970. I treated it like a diary stimulated by the events of my life, using whatever came to mind about Scotland through the circumstances of work, reading and travel. The surreal style is no merit, I expect, but it emerged as the only way to be brief, dense and serious. The captions were sometimes added later, and are meant to work like the titles of poems. The verse interludes are more flexible work, and might be read as punctuation points.

CONTENTS

1

THE VIOLENCE OF EXILE

THE PASSPORT

Cleaning out old junk, I find
My father's passport, with his picture
Smudged with ink. The mauve-pink paper,
My name signed in his neat writing,
Eden's name there, make it strange.

He used it once, went on business
To Dusseldorf the year of Munich,
Brought me back a clockwork donkey
I still have and saw the war
Coming, which he fought in. Turning

The stiff pages in my hands, I almost
Feel his long-boned hands again
Over my child's hands. I wonder
What he'd think of my passport,
Wine-stained, full of stamps, uncancelled?

His eyes, questioning, look out
From under brushed-back hair. This man will
Never know I've been to Munich
Nor that our side won the war
Between our two journeys, our

Two lives. This draughtsman, born
At Overton in Lanarkshire
Late in 1904, whose height
It says is five foot nine, whose eyes
Are hazel, hair dark brown, is dead.

1

Oatcakes

They come in a high tin, cylindrical, sealed with cellophane. Each night, sometime after eleven, I come downstairs into the kitchen and reach up for it. In a corrugated tube of paper, dished a little, and resting in each other like the bowls of spoons, they confront the eye with the solidity of porridge. When I was little, I used to know the thicker ones as bannocks. These are neither one thing nor the other, they rest in between, perhaps nearer the norm than the cheaper varieties I remember before the war. Those were brittle triangles in folded paper. These are medallions, rough shields. Targes, almost. If Bruce were to come back now in fire along the glen, he could seize one to his arm again and win that famous battle. Bannockburn. The apotheosis of oatmeal.

2

Bagpipes

Their sound is perhaps the only one I know that works in the stomach. It comes like a hard meat, stringy with gristle. For anyone who was born in the scattered landscape it summons and governs, there is no escaping its bitter, outmoded rallying-cry. More than the drab gauds of Caledonia they still flaunt in for Burns suppers and tourism, it steams and twitches in the cauldron of belonging, the long vault of Celtic exile. Every man who hears it is a king in the blood, returned out of the foreign slime to renew his dead alliance.

3

Scottish Terrier

He was bustling along with his head to the paving-stones, aware as they all are of the delicate world of smell that swirls below knee-level. On a frayed leather lead he roamed, strayed, and returned, as black as a

5

chopped swathe of coal from an abandoned face in Lanark. Inside his squared axe of a muzzle, the chipped eyes flew and coasted, humorous, maybe a little dour, sure of the bleak weather and the soft South.

4

Scottish

If it were just a matter of words, no doubt we should all fall in the gap between *skittish* and *sottish*. We have the dry wit of the fairies, a touch fey and feline, and we cross it with the dream of blood like clear water from the rocks, potent as Strathisla. Somewhere in the space between dancing like angels on pins, and lying face down in the flooded brook of the arteries, we live, rise, and dwindle, miraculous as centaurs in the double-nature of Highland and Lowland. Elsewhere the pincers close. Here it is all division, *Scottish* into twin bits.

5

Scotch

As for that other word, already ennobled in a world coinage of wanting, how shall we all deny there is gold and honey, maple and pure syrup, in the pure malt? If this were what it meant to be of it, a long race would engender in the bowels of Finland, St. Lucia and Paraguay, no more known to the forgotten corners of the loch-spitted anvil we call Scotland than butter-scotch, or scotched snakes.

6

Sir Walter Scott

I saw him once under the hammer. In all that gold and red tooling, so many volumes of foundered power, reduced to the final inelegance of dismissive auction. He wrote himself in these last journals of the sun setting, the bark out at sea in the dark, with the keel leaking. Here in

the dust, with the worms working, I finger over the ells of such sunk
grandeur that tears come.

7

A Concrete Poet

I see him with his gentle eyes, writing in the cramped room we shared in
Budapest. The words come again in the iron pages of a quarterly,
carved, exact, wry in the grain of a pine or a bog-oak. Not the same.
Other words. In the irony of a frivolous Christmas I read them out like
maggots, weeded from the dented slab he engraved them in, precious
ink riding on a grey plateau. *Space insects found in Great Bear*. In the
famine of European honour, whittling a few ears of local fame to a
flame of plenty, I see him as far advanced in exile as I am, in his own
land.

8

The Idea of Scotland as a Scattered Universal

Somewhere in that man with a name like a pirate captain, Willard van
Orman Quine, there extrudes an anchor, a hook through to the under-
lying nexus. There in the concept of universals as everywhere, as
disintegrated, as finalities, I come into the gut's truth of Scotland. Here,
in the South, four hundred miles from the Cannongate, the intrinsic
resonance still aims and thunders out of the fur of dogs, the meal of
food, the vowels even of converts. Shatter and split it how you will, it
veers and collapses, triumphing, viridical, and as prevalent as the dirt
under nails. In the North it intensifies and thickens. Here it is all
diffusion, adulterate with water, occasional only. And yet it teases, like
tartan, like Burns. I follow it, as the will o' the wisp.

9

Kippers

Grained black and gold, as if scalded from an incandescence of Arctic
marble, they appear hewn, slabbed here. In a striped apron, joking,
with three sons as Cockney as he is, the market-man levers them up in
bled-white knuckles, hurls them in scales, vends them. Amidst so much
from the cold rings that lap Wick and Iona, these are delivered entire in
salt. Others emerge as foreign, enlarged visitors, opaque-eyed from the
shawls at the sea's bottom. These come with the sour credentials of
Camerons, apostles. I taste their hacked veins, alert with the sprigs of
imaginary parsley. As much slapped fish out of water as they are, I pass
through in the rain, touting baskets.

10

My Father's Compasses

If I touch them, whenever it is, now even, the kinetic rigour of allowed
grief would still stir, demand its obol. To be reflecting, even, forgetful
of the proper honours, not entering as if like a celebrant to the echoing
hall, cold on white boards, not reaching up for the brass hangers,
dragging the strained mahogany open, wrenching the scarred pack from
its blue wrappers, easing off the elastic, feeling over the tools, unrusted,
locked in velvet, already betrays, quibbles. Another night, in another
mood, the drawer will open. Now I write only the words: *compasses, he
was a draughtsman*.

11

The Book So Far

Pausing now, I begin to count the lines. Only four hundred still. After
the third day, driving with blunt carbon for whatever lies beyond the
racing black points in the darkness, I feel the North stir like something

at the bottom of a loch, dredged up, as with eels, into the blinding triviality of revealed print. For a moment it seems, again, pointless to advance, even to contemplate such absurdity. And then I am still writing, fighting beyond the obstruction, the blockage, as into a new terrain where the weed may clear, the amazing monster fleer its twin necks out of the water, the resolved synthesis, or miniature insight, quicken to a firm head.

12

Stevenson

In Samoa, lolling amidst such explicit state, I see him as prodigal beyond all curing. In morning calm, beside the intense clarity of the water, I reach to touch the unwaxed ends of his characteristic moustache, lanker, less ginger, than mine. In a dream of light-houses, those founded towers, he hears the long fog-horn of ancestry re-echo in the chambers of his bowels, disintegrating into splinters of diarrhoea, excoriating unease, nausea. What did it mean to be the pineapple of industrial power, and yet so dedicated to the palpable margins, at least in *their* eyes? We all know it, allowed only the persistence of miniature commitment, though wasting still, under that belligerence of determined vanity, urge for show-manship, to be the king. I recognise it, admire, am afraid of it. Wastrel in elegance, he beckons, admonishes.

13

The Thriller Writers

As in Raeburn's portrait of The Two Archers, enigmatic, half-intrinsic to the arc suspended between the bow-string and the bent yews, they leap out, smiling, the two faces. Buchan's. Fleming's. If one is to drive, surmounting the other, into a frail lead, as horses, racing against the current of blocking air, towards fame, money, it might be Tweedsmuir's. Neck ahead by the edge of appropriate honours, anchoring the English empire as securely as Kipling. Later it flails, tail fluke in the squirm of dependent vassals, into the beached vortex of Southern Florida, the playfields of Bond, emergent over the shirred eggs and the waffles. Half-Scotsmen, androgynous heroes of mid-cult, they amaze, worry, and flicker, ghostly candles over the vault of fiction. Close behind them in the waxed air, I hear Byron chuckle, the cracked knuckles of the bad Lord.

14

Echoes of Ice-Cream

During the war it was snow-freeze, I remember the nougat wafers in Peter Equi's. Now there is no deception, the real ice emerges in the double prices of lesser helpings. Or else the mind, as the eye and hand have shrunk, has expanded, blown up the past wafers to a privileged excess. Who knows? I doubt that Peter does, or his rival Tony across the road, long buried in the ascendancy of the centre, the supermarketeers with their whippsies and water-blocks.

15

Holidays on the Clyde

That was Ardrossan, where the paddle-boat struck out across the levelled steel for Arran. I remember the brass-studded rail, black hills plucked out of reach like the slides in a lantern lecture. Shivering in a scratch wind, with a wartime collar up against the intrusion of chill and water, I could almost cry for boredom. In the mind, legends of a wet thriller in a gothic unit, week-ended off by storm or winter, struggled, were aborted, flailed away in the creamed stern spume from the twin wheels. Gulls would be circling, flat-out, scissored, amazed by the human dream of a day's air in the rain blazing. Then it would dock, and the hard walk through the squared wall-flowers, the clocks and the treacle-scones, would begin. I shiver for it, even here, in the safe distraction and torture of London, freed by labour from the suicide of entertainment.

16

The Bulletin

Squared like the *Mirror*, it slapped through the letter-gap at Kinburn
with the regularity of a wag-clock. On the inside pages the incessant
Tatlerish weddings glazed the rough paper with bridal smiles, honey of
anticipated marital bliss in the holes and bunkers of an Ayr retreat.
Sensual veilings, flapped pockets, those hard-edged Jedburgh faces
thrust from the doors of Humbers. And then through the bustle of
other news to the strips, and *Tammy Troot*, with that faint smell of
lavender-water in my cousin's cousin's name.

17

Rothesay

In that estuary of abrupt splendour, bourgeois as drop-scones, the wind
hits the attentive steamers, rocking at their moorings by jetties, posts.
On a squalled route between the tea-rooms and the floral tributes, with
old men playing clock-golf, and the women, be-hatted, gossipy, ranged
in bap-formations across the park-seats, I am promenading, a sterile six
year old with my hand in Evelyn's. Her serious face, framed in bell-hair,
accosts the casual snapper's eye as we pause in our blazers. I can almost
feel the length of my child's lashes when I blink. The album smells
slightly, with age.

18

Thinking About the Book So Far

Having moved, perhaps, from the impedimenta of a general notion, one
is at it acutely, informed by those bits of a more personal vision that
survive. In a trice Largs fits to Rothesay, the long stag's head of
Scotland has been whittled short to the brazen popular boomerang of
the Clyde. So many long days rocked on it, wasting through school-

holidays. It makes the guilt come, nourishes the grief in aspic. I feed on it, as on a fuel.

19

My Mother's Hand-Bag

So again I try, this time with my fingers in the crocodile skin of the youngest daughter's last bag. Its scent of powder is acrid now, as of burnt cordite, not Coty. I remember the top-hatted over-cases, tight-sliding to cover the floury drums, replete with the mother-perfume, woman-odour of a late 1920's romance, pervasive as sepia. I choke with the mingled fat and wine of sib-ship.

20

Quarrels

If it were family only, that feuding liaison-change, interceding through cut moquette amidst spent whispers, rustle of death-smell, granny's dresses dragging, that would be understood, or at least understandable. What makes it stranger, less open, is the dowelled bitterness, wormed in, as if aboriginal ratchets through dour winters had set the screws for it. Is this Pictish foraying, as if crossing walls, what it is to be Scots?

21

Haggis

Never eaten without a shudder, spiced, originate in the black mirk of a witchcraft conveniently forgotten, they squat, knotted, horny, reluctant to be moved, behind the soil's glass of the delicatessen counter. They seem to crouch, crawl almost. With the alacrity of toads, they approach tables, gathered in strong moments by the clenched hands of aspirant foreigners. Whenever nationals touch them, they wilt, like toadstools. On a fey night, with a sliver of moon squeezed over the gables, trolls and ninnies flirt out from the chimney-alcoves to sup and gobble on them. Visceral groin-ropes, warty commanders, brute eggs. I ignore the potato-grey nudge of their lights against my eye-balls. As at vegetable-billiards, they pot roots, clay-reds. No-one is able for them.

22

My Father's Belongings

To be touring in the monuments of agnostic grandeur, those dunked egg-shells of an adolescent bereavement! How can I stroll back so often, sucking the pursed arrogances of my own nihilism, more than a quarter of a century after the lighter was struck for the last time? In flame and alienation, I become miniature, am an entrant. Where will it end, who will take over, what will pursue me? I feel enacted, verbal, conscious only of the self-abnegating need to be dutiful, not let go the taut bulldog's-tooth grip on the iron remnants. Armoured in these, as in a loyal conscience, I re-enter the world, easier for them. The drawer closes, musty in cerements, eclectic in all it offers: honour, purpose, vitality.

23

My Mother

When she struck the liver with her hammer, the frost came. No beautiful
girl was kept in the airing-cupboard, alert for her son, only the paying-
guest in the room with the iron table-shelter, the spinster headmistress
who said you "grew out of" Flecker. Turned into stone, though, by the
imbalance of loving-nature, she walked a hundred yards to her place in
the ground. There I stand over her, with my handful of daffodils,
feeling the line ending. Her strong arms are as young and warm as a
man's. She preserved the last ounce of German blood in the cauldron of
Shotts. Out of the mine, the clans call.

24

The Idea of Scotland

Perhaps the difficulty lies in the transition: slipping between the
interstices of imagined fragments, anticipated moments, aching to be
free-running again. Feeling the creeping miasma of its improbable
presence, leaking South from Carter Bar. In the long sickness of absence,
the general essence of Scotland rusts, is inevitably a puissant reminder,
a wound. I feel the twinge of it. Its lips mouth the approaches, become
a welter of renewal. I bleed towards them through *Billy Budd*, ripping
screens from the onion's eye of the EKCO.

25

Driving North on the A1

On the road in the glare's pupil, blazing through the corona of
England's edges, how far it all seemed from the known, financed
purposes! To be tucking that black stick, immaculate as a dandy's cane,
in the rubber-laced gate of the synchro-mesh, was a motorized
reduction, a grinding towards knowledge, a thrown change in the

gambling-wheel of imagination. I fled North, away from the fear of it
all failing.

26

Thinking About the Book

Always this writing about writing, is that Scottish? The drain of
ambition, intelligence, all potency to a soured inturning head, a bitten

toe-nail. One hates the terminology, the insistence of it. Hoisting all islands, via ducts and carousals to a pin's jag of raw carbon, friably rubbed. Abusing one's own jars of imbibed oxygen, ore-stuff, and all for a mere glow in the margin, a few hundred words.

27

Thinking about My Birth-Place

Even to have touched Shotts on the map, sheared off all thought of a visit, or *not this time*, rejects, is a kind of panacea for, some kind of penetration. I bore in my mind, as through the doors of a lost valley, towards what dinosaurs, elaborate fossil kingdoms, men with foreheads of hay. It is all Doyle, swimming-pools, miner's facilities. No white house looms in the jungle, clean as a serving-cloth, or a Sunday napkin. The snow-faced inhabitants are all so far off. They dissolve in their own glitter, brittle as tinsel, fire-crinkled. I cry out for them, for one of them. He reaches — I think he reaches — to halt a child's hand on a dog's ear. The shot rings like a shell in the sheep's brain of my own muzzled recollection.

28

My Surname

What does it mean *Malbeatha*? Named from before the Normans broke the English with cavalry, before the arrow ground into Harold's eye, am I the child of a real notion, or only as dredged and shallow as a faked artery-tree? No, there is something. There is the name. Blood is a tortuous current, woven below rock and heather in the salmon-streams and the sewer. Syllables alter, but the name's essence grips through eleven centuries, facing pit-props in the worm's tunnel of nothingness. Here is a link, a bit of silver, a brooch reeking with cattle-piss. I kiss it in salt, am its owner.

29

My Christian Name

To be George? Is that nothing? I dislike it, its hint of *Georgic*, rustic as
bees. Too stupid, bumbling, to be a firm name. And too redolent of the
Georges, the end of the Jacobite expectations in the white noise of the
45. I hear the death-rattle of cockades, teeth shivered in the skull's
volcano of Skye. For a king, to go in drag, was that worse? I am
Georgian, cautious, a bitter Capricorn, signed under the bow-sprit of
the goat, whatever I say.

2

THE NOSTALGIA OF RETURN

THE LANDING

Before the frigate's mast the freshening wind
    Swept scented with the firs. The crowned son watched
The Northern lights illumine his long wound
    In furrowed water, and the moon bewitched

His wake to Ireland. So the cause advanced
    In brilliance, furled in purple, to the shore
And forty clansmen waded — none convinced
    Their king should anchor — to the wooden share

Driven into flowing marble. Who could tell
    If the weird light would settle on the rock
For Christian royalty, or the bell toll
    And the sword flicker by the burning rick

Only to bury them? That crib of fire
    Burned when the foreign axe-men drove their keels
Through cliffs of bone, and sisters crouched in fear
    Lifting the pinched cross to their wimpled skulls

With white blood running. How could those dead nuns
    Nourish the light in their cold flesh and land
When the long night was turning to the Nones?
    Beside the levers of the sea they lined

The sighing gunwales. Far away the drum
    Beat from Iona where the stones were broken,
The papers burned. And here their following dream
    Shivered and went to ground beneath the bracken

With the bones of sheep. And when the drooping herd
    Hang by the loch like falls of weeping willow,
Masters of rock and forest shall be hired
    For Lowland shillings, and the reckling wallow

In the earl's castle, and the king must die
   In water *so the legend ran, bleak rock*
Lying in state for that consuming day
   When the white dog shall rise below the wreck

And tear the props loose to confound the globe
   In slaughter, and the king, past kneeling men,
Stride into honour on his native glebe,
   And the swell die, with a slow sobbing moan.

30

Leaving Bishop Auckland

Ounce-eyed in the chill morning, humping suit-cases to fit snug to the khaki Italian general's boot of the Scimitar, it was almost an imposition, a task. On the road to Corbridge, the air cleared. As we ran between bare moors, the annihilating lightning of an Aston Martin passed. Sun behind bars began to break through over touching hedges, frayed rock. In the burnt-out cow-parsley, reared feet high, there were acres of that off-maroon weed that used to flower on bomb-sites. As driven, the mind flew, was ahead.

31

At Carter Bar

Where those hard staves, axe-headed, foretold and drove home the victory, amidst height, wind, and the breathless heirs of cattle-thieves, bitter horse-flies hissed and cannonaded. As if dog-fought, one fell, blitzed the cream of my arm. Annulled blood, the itch of centuries, drummed under its teeth's hooves. As it hovered, swung the black screw of its tail above spent ichor, the ichonography of history leapt into soft focus. Blurred hills, visiting wives, all droned and slept in oblivious thistles, blue spikes of the dream. A spray of heather dropped from a grill plastered with the wings of butterflies. In anxiety, I touched Scotland where all it meant was sleep, and the dregs of beer-bottles.

32

Jedburgh

It is all extravagant violence and echoes, like a girl feeding a Pyrenean with a bone. In the mind-grinding of mixed boilings, Jethart snails, a certain granitic sweetness binds with these hung carcases to a tough splendour. Here they anticipated the Scots, here we ate rhubarb tart.

For present sweets, cruel assizes: irony of bottled heads, vizors in moth-balls. I confront each boned fish-nose with a circumspect attention.

33

Melrose Abbey

Amidst fretted stone, enlacing the wide sky beside the hills twinned by a spell, it breathes, emits the odour of lobellia, goldenrod. Abused reds, abandoned oranges, meretriciousness of an agonized yellow, all gather, submit, ease to one French electrified pattern of beds, lawns, ruins. Here monks paced, eyed the clouds for a rain sign: here Michael Scott, wizard *extraordinaire*, was put to his nightly toil in occupying that industrious demon. Whoever sees it, him, by moonlight, is assured of a grave in this wilderness of sandstone.

34

Scott's Toys at Abbotsford

Under glass, it all comes to a head: apotheosis of trivia, collector's brittle exotica. Nailed by the hems, edges, of his massive existence, Napoleon's cloak-clasps, brass flies, filched from his chariot, oppose the ball of oatmeal, nest-like, unearthed in a dead soldier's pocket on Culloden Moor. Here Byron's ring, the Prince's snuff-box, Rob Roy's purse and dagger, instil some momentary pride in the founded posterity of Scotland, the available descended relics. I stand to attention for them in my sentimental belly. Outside an unprecedented sun hammers a few shadows into paving-stones like tablet, and a giant's thistle, over six feet high, repels a charabanc of French tourists with their lenses and T-shirts. Outside his last clothes now, the great writer whose hand never cooled on the pen, drifts like a breeze across his own bronze death-mask, at peace, and unread. The arms rest on the wall, thumb-screws in the smoking-corridor, with the half-height gates for his dogs. I hear a gas-jet flare, as a ghost's hand draws the chain above the writing table. He made his own light, that final confidence of a talent striding in the shadow of greatness. Power, acceptance, fame: to supply one's own gas, entertain kings, and know William Wordsworth.

35

Edinburgh

So much changed. George Square gone under the hammer, auctioned off to make room for a new brutalism. Within the iron skeleton of the Royal Scottish Museum, as in an airship, the delicious twist of fountains, erotica, Chinese fire-arms; and then re-arrangements, a hint of trouble in *Mining*, exhibited *Pomp*, so many unveiled and roped-off possibilities. I sense again their onset like a shrill wind, seeing the past more clear than stones.

36

Scottish Pound Notes

After quarrelling over prices, the commitment of rooms, one lies under the anaesthesia of Radio One, washed, in pyjamas, acres of light falling on carpeted flowers. If the heating fails, the piano tips in the street, red men with inhuman foreheads burst in to demand impossible ransom, there are always these, although miniature, crisp still, and as patriotic as leaves. I crease them between midnight fingers, eased of rings, naked and open with them. What levels of unbegotten trouble we slough off in the presence of money! Scottish as kilts, flags, they adore pressure, accept, resist it, as granite as walls. What goes on behind them is their affair. I only ask their connivance, as all do, in the day to day running of deceitfulness, an engendered separation and soldering of relationships. We pay our way out, as in. All national currency is one's accomplice. With their bridges and thistles, these notes are mine.

37

Edinburgh

To have obtained regress against high charges, is an affair of import,
exhilaration, and especially on an August sabbath. I drive from the
coarse emptiness of your suburbs, float on a bath of sun towards the
Forth Bridge, and then plummet, violined through taut strung
catenaries behind oil-lorries. Moaning brakes of one, women with
crushed straw hats in all colours, remind me of Queensferry. So, to the
air-machine, the avenue of mid-morning.

38

Birnam Wood

If it ever came, as it does now, in limited waves across bare slopes, like a
monk's tonsured skull, it would only be primitive larches, forgotten ash
leaves, diminutive rowans. In all those crimson berries, ripped open to
put their tongues out, I re-enter the mockery of the legend. As rooks
wheel in a cloud-wrack, instructive diminuendos of clattering thistles
empurple a prospect of much reduced sublimity. It is all resonances,
vanished supremacy, book-learning. Even the remote name of the castle,
half an inch away on the map, is an echo of stupidity. *Dunce. Inane.*
The puns lock and rattle.

39

Above Pitlochry

I begin to study, Indian-squatting on a tufted knoll, the impermanence
of thistles, their exquisite colour-balance against the miles of grouse-
moor, inveterate heather. Drinking *Fergora*, I hear a genie wail in the
depths of the bottle. Not more than a mile from here, the author of
Thrawn Janet foxed a quill. A man with a tall hat, strapping a pack on
his back, hails the pair of us with a nod, as he lopes by, demon-meat.

On these moors, you would throw your left shoe in the wind on
principle, be assured of averting something.

40

Water Before The Devil's Elbow

Sliding over lush moor-grass, away from a ghost dozing in a *Herald*,
I consider what annunciations of crossed swords are extrapolated in the
far tinkle of the brook, lacing clean pebbles with a skein of precise
motion. I bend on my knees like a boy-soldier, axeable with head down
to the cataract over a step-stone. Here on the plank bridge, besieged by
a slow catarrh of midges, one awaits the inevitable rusticity of pimples,
genetic itch, rich disorder amidst sock-falls. I piss afar, blistering
scorched heather-knots with a hissing barley-sugar stick of irreverent
urine, bladder-wrack.

41

A Flushed Grouse

It ran, high-necked, like an Arizona road-runner, across the A8,
anchoring the brushed wheels to the verge in astounded rigour. In
flapping, screech-notes rising to a pibroch of thin concern, it was
fast-off, low across hedges as all eye-barrels aligned, fired. They feed on
heather, exclude sheep, are a flared élite. I divide one, am its only
begettor. The brown wings expand and are downed into flattened
hedge-hogs, wrenched cats, a bazooka-range of shelled rabbits.

42

On the Constipation of Ideas

Somehow, after four hours of this greyness, in positioned readiness
along the quays of a granite forbearance, I sense again the force-meat,
the stuffing of it. Such elephantine monoliths of an after-dinner

evacuation, a vowel-movement! As flat pats, cattle-sloughed: corded bombs and balls, out of sheep's eatings: it all stiffens, is corrugated, then flows. In the dysentery of a sympathetic affliction, one's mother-country is taken in, digested. It emerges reared into grey blocks, is a Union Street of phantasmal hyphens, cubes of hay-words.

43

Losing A Number-Plate: Thoughts on Disguise

It broke, severed, was in the dust. Perhaps to have driven yards, miles, days even, with a vehicle losing its own identity, was enough. Screws loosen, a slab of pistachio granite reckons, hacks: and, rapastrat!, the available number is torn clear, the mind separated from its conscience. As with a beard, or a stocking over the face of tenderness, the Campbell or train-robber will strike, abuse descended hospitalities. I muse amidst the irritabilities of garages.

44

Aberdeen: The Quay

I remember the Regent quay in the darkness, and the three masts of the ghost-ship at its moorings. On the left were the loose bales of Norwegian or Inverness wood, their scent as a strong wind in the cold. Somewhere in the hold a light was burning. A man with a pipe came up and was gone, amidst tar-smells, an infusion of beeriness. There were few sounds, only the creak of tackle and brass, the faint rattle of cutlasses, or rigging. Beside the Q store, windows vaguely packed with warm socks and jeans, gloves and sea-jackets, a drunkard yawed in a burn of silver light. This was the first night I had been so far North in the kingdom.

The Fish-Market: Aberdeen

Waking, sprawled as in a meringue, amidst huge pillows, it appeared a crass project, a vulgarising. And then out in a khaki shirt into the crisp wind, confronting benevolence of a foreign morning sunshine, notices in Swedish, men in rubber boots. It was all sliding, toboggans over ice, ice crushed amidst gutted mackerel, gashed necks, revealed innards, wet splay of skate on the cobbles. The star diopside of a gull's beady eye, downcurving beak, rashing holes in a siege of ditched herring. Their hacking cries, hatcheted rough gaps in the air. Sellers, walkie-talkies and flying baskets. I racketeered through them, abruptly sick, scunnered by the ripple of slow profit.

46

Banff: A Public Holiday

As when they boarded the *Marie Celeste*, cutlery lay ready on the boards, here there were cars at the kerbs, engines running almost, except there was no sound in the silence, the sudden enveloping noon-day oblivion. From mansard windows, no gauze faces peered, hands poised. In the leather sustenance of being an alien, pacing, as if with fingers tensed above imaginary guns, I walked in the square, beside the red mine, the cannon. Considered a house for sale, paused by a linoleum-chandler, ate mince and broth in a plastic room with a wurlitzer, chose Fleetwood Mac, was absorbed in the stunned quiet of it by the posters of American beauty spots, the camp insouciance of the owner. That was all, except for a gallon of petrol, a dry walk on the whirling shore amidst the shells.

47

Cullen

Under the tiers of indigenous granite, thrown round a bend like a stone, initiative flirted with the sea's brevity, the afternoon of strapwrack and pebbles. I ramped on a rock, flew in the face of history with a dog's medal, joined the crew of a rope, tugging snails in a sand-castle. Mysterious free lava of dozing in the sheltered arm-pits of a stinking resort. There is coal everywhere, even in the eyes of breeding deerhounds. Here it is open-cast, exploring a section of *having a holiday on the shore*.

48

The Elgin Museum

Imagine a packing-case in a field. Arrange it with a balustrade of mahogany, arch its back over shrunken heads, a crouched Incan mummy, coffin-boards and electrics. Here is your case of the fourteen British owls, not all named, and your stuffed Scottish cat, that miniature tiger. There is your coracle, your John Martin, your iron-age canoe dug from a bog. With Ramsay Macdonald's privy letters for coy measure, the charters and Mayan figurines explore their own destiny with aplomb. They have a chance now, it will grow to a 2/- entrance, a man with a peaked cap: they will sack the courteous aged woman, have proper tickets, make teas in the Pictish bull's corner, become famous.

49

The Site of Culloden

To have come, at evening, along this grim road, sombre in the twilight of a late summer, was a pilgrimage to a lost Mecca. By the blood-ditch, and where McGillivray fell, dredging some legendary pretensions of heroism from the salt-marsh, I am sad amidst firs, pines, heather. An absentee rain is in the thin dripping along the panes of my mind, the soft voices, the sheltering of matches, car-engines. That stone, for instance, for the *mixed clans*. What is it, there especially, that is drinking forgotten emotion from a neep-glass of reticence? I try to touch the forehead of an Ayrshire calf, driven like a stake through the barbed wire: a stranded cairn barks fierce and glum at once. Between the stones where the Prince and Cumberland guaged war with glasses, a spirited blood-shed had happened in forty minutes. And about 1500 gentlemen, many of them fatigued Highlanders, lay down for ever in the grass. That was the last battle ever fought in these islands. Even now, the tourists walk away dejected, as if defeated.

50

Inverness

Dismissed from two hotels, I eat thin broth in the third. Above a car-park, or what they would call at Banff a *motor stance*, neon gloss adds glitter to the pewtered mirror of the river in the sinking sun's light. I remember Elgin's *Lazarus Lane*, am resurrected by the pudding-thoughts of tomorrow. Wick burns in the church of the future, is waxed and rounded.

51

Coffee at Aultnamain Inn

After riding between moors, a little punished by the endurance of maroon, one is briefly elated, halted by the white dazzle, remote roofs. Closer, it becomes Highland cattle, digging blind furry muzzles into marsh, floods and geese, lichen along the hems of walls. Inside, amidst clocks duelling, a dinner-gong upheld by elephants, confronted table-ware, I stroke the bald otter, relieved of the need to feed umbrellas, canes to his bow. After skinned coffee, bills of a low clearance, refreshed attack on the sky-line, amazing indifference to vans. We pelt North.

52

Thoughts In A Public School, Once The Seat of the Sutherlands

Suppose those abused boys, chilled by the spittle of Michaelmas, revolted in the changing-rooms. What a flurry of curled rolls from *The Indispensable*, foghorn explosiveness from the tipped porcelain basins, grave reduction of vaults, cat-skins! I observe in a flea's cranny, snug above elm and conkers, the particular squashed re-alignment of prep-rooms, mysterious Jacobite relics, bread from the siege of Paris. Even the gaelic duke, master of the cats, could hardly stem the lightning of encircled geraniums, thrown breakage-books. It would all be wrecked, unrestorable.

53

Recalling Pods on the Broom at Culloden

When you snap one open, the interior is an olive canoe, without rowlocks. Only the two sloe nuts are in place, unreckoned in the taut annals of musterings. One breaks loose, cracking as the black shell does, in a sloughed skein of fire. All over the moor, such powder-blackened thunders are abruptly stifled, roused, gnashed, and aborted. In the season, witches ride them like harriers, white rapists. They scream their cockade-hue, one fusilade of remote pride.

54

Shopping and Visiting the Shore at Brora

I buy victuals, as if for an Arctic voyage, amidst the almost Chinese courtesies of reluctant stores. There are chocolate snow-balls, arranged cheeses, a pat of embroidered butter. So many mistresses of a general destiny, outstaring poor incomes for chimes and wine. I descend through the smells of bananas, tarred rope. On a strange grass — perhaps more of a cactus, it stores water, flourishes between the weed and the marram — I pore for an explanation of why it is so easy to live between two furnaces, the ear of the shells, breath of cows.

55

Brochs

They were built in the line of a daft eddy, electric scoops of a 2nd century technology more expert than wattle. One of them stands here, rocked to the ground. I hear a plucked harp amusing itself with the hair of a demon. Stone lintels, a cosmodrop of nettles. In the thick wind, *soup de jour* of whatever Brora calls elevenses, grappling hand-holds from the lights of a doomed refectory, I gulp legend like eel's broth. In the distance a rose machine massacres hay.

56

Mist on the Road to Thurso

After days of alien smoothness, it comes up out of the flat sea beyond the green ball of Dounreay, synoptic, alizarine, tenacious as snails. No screen wiper entirely clears it, it frets the edges, a tasselled magnificence in the cow's tail of a rainfall. I sweep through, ongoing towards Thurso, pursued by the vigilance of a blue jeep. In the drear curtain of whatever Caithness ails with, flung humps of a dumpling-laden soup-scape engross the whole left. On the right, there is nothing, grey nothing, advancing in full sail to beach its forty keels in the nun-soil of what will later be the esplanade.

57

Thurso

As one book said it, perhaps the Shell one, it was here we reached the last ripples. Where the stone flung into the brook of European culture by Michael Angelo foundered, its currents lapsed to these boundaries.

Beyond rock, sandstone, the mussels, patellae, razor-shells extenuate a more gothic union. Here the even ridges, plain glass, mathematics within the dominion of reason, retch, stagger, but maintain a final equilibrium on the pitching decks of Thorfinn. Today, along bare renewed slums, a white spume races, magnetic to the tracers of failing *Starfighters*. Fumbling towers, mill-shaped, exact a hint of flour, are a mediaeval touch. The iron bandstand is echoing *Rule Britannia*. Lobster-pots drain into mud.

58

Chambered Cairns

If there had been anything, beyond the smirr of fret on the rear-view mirrors, it would have relieved the battle-tension of ripped levis, hooked on a calthrop of wire. Instead, there was only a van reversing, sludge over top-shoes, in the sudden total recall of a county one third of which is bog. Elsewhere, there is death in the upright slabs of flags, Caithness fudge. Here it is echoes, transistors of impertinent sub-culture, views through torn hedge. So much for the nautilus, these chambered shells would surprise no-one.

59

The Lighthouse at Dunnet Head

All night I had heard its crabbed voice in the darkness, pulsations of glue-sound through solid wind and air. Here in the death-white mist flowing, the white heads lifted their veiled horns to the guess of ships, lowing for the milk of recognition. A huge immaculate generator through an open door, all red paint and polished copper, with a loose handle vibrating, fed them with shovelled love. In the icicle the light lay in, twisted through the sugar-stick of stairs, people were plying like tugs. Breathless in the glass incinerator, where the touched correct clock moved, sure above its brass key, the enormous glacier of guaged reflectors arced in its dish of mercury as easy as bells over hard polish. From these four central lenses, grouped as the compass points, the beam broke across tentative sea, enlarged from a paraffin lamp. So much effect from so little means, economy of the clear mind's expression! Here over iron Edwardian grids, the children of Stevenson propped their eyelids with knitting, never read on pain of dismissal, kept the light in. I felt the giddy, psychedelic rainbow of intentional magnification enter my brain, spin the world to a shipwrecked mote in the sun's delirium. Here was the glaring central core of Scotland, the meaningful clan's oath of a known destiny, to save ships, the imperilled few on whatever seas boiled in the vast wake of the grave. Beside its roots, a pet kestrel spun his blue eye, screeching on the greased string of a tied security. As I touched his breast, the selective beak hooked to my thumb, though in patience, dreadful. The car backed and turned to the South. This was the farthest point of the land-mass, the spearhead of the United Kingdom.

60

John O'Groats Hotel

So here was the reputed end, the initial steps in all cross-country running and walking races, the dead North beating against its rubbish and barriers. Flotsam, detritus of fabulous shells, amazing crazed areas of crushed sherds. In the horns of the twin sitting-rooms, expectant relieved hikers dispute for postcards, television. A man mends the set with the grace of queen mothers. Tonight there will be news again, a grey film of escapist hurry across the kipper-fields. Meanwhile, they dunk Abernethy biscuits in mixed coffee, spout their intelligent loyalties to respective teams, ache with walking in golf-joints.

61

Wick

To be lit by the name of a candle, flame in the side-burns of Caledonia's jaw-fissure, reduce pounds by the hundred thousand to a trash of slime. Fate of a village betrayed by its airport, adjusted to foreign landings, dukes in the abstract creels of high-wing monoplanes. Each lands, evacuates and retires. Pursued by a Hellespont of shoals and ghillies, they head North. In a vacuum of pies, I follow in third, razing the dewy grass for a parking throne. One has to keep up with the Hanovers.

62

Tea at the Aultnamain Inn

I will pause to consider the North British character, its repetitions, its nuances. How, for example, a spare couple will digress a little, and prefer sly tea with scones in Syra, or Altnahara, to a rich repast in Elgin. As, on the present refreshed occasion, two such receded through old known moorland to what was called the Aultnamain Inn. There they ate white scones, domed Madeira cake, and a sort of rare wrapped wafer. I see them wash their jam-stained fingers, dry with care in the paper-towels, appraise the three clocks with their hourly chimes. It has the air of an annual visit. Now they are filled, pay, nod. They re-mount their intended photograph, their Scimitar, to ride on.

63

Thinking About the Loch Ness Monster at Fort Augustus

Below the cypress-trees, on the stone verandah of the sixth lock, they walked as towards a fate in some ring. Nervous amidst toadstools, they heard twigs divide in two, stones throw themselves into empty moments and drown. Where the green caravans of the Investigation slept in muddle, a round fog-lamp flushed a trough in the dark throat of whatever was coughing silently, or not coming. As it went on doing so, they stood arm in arm with the skeletons of old-fashioned fish, two low grins near to the parked loch, still flat and hissing from the delicate ruffle of winds. Later, they returned, humbled. Nothing had happened.

64

Beside Loch Lochy

Squatting again, as an ancestor must have done, I felt the chill water with my right forefinger, as if in a ritual purification of something. Far up the fire-breaks in the forests, I imagined concealed hosts lay, toasting the king beyond the water, the bringer of spells. In a passing wind, I shivered among arriving deck-chairs, felt the menace in the title *Elf* as a small maroon car paused. Old people are all there is room for in Scotland.

65

The Museum at Fort William

Escaped from the toss of humanity, for a shilling one buys a reprieving of idleness. Under kirk ladles, a black sickness wells. One is up to one's knees in syrup of it. A blear abstract, oiled length of distortion they call the "disguised" view of the Prince, itches at the corners of a leased irritation, waylaying anger. A few tourists in caps and gumboots are aghast at winnowing sieves, flails. In the other room, assured of a rufus hatred, the Aluminium monarchy rips the ninth veil from its secrets. These are the cores of pans, wires, a bumper on a *Vitesse*, the sacrificial anodes preserving ships' hulls from corrosive electrolyte. As in all museums, at last the agnostic prettiness of it sets in, revolts. Upstairs, in a simulated croft, a wizened gnome in a mutch cards wool, is the bull's eye of one's last fears.

66

Remembering an Art Gallery

All day I remember the great paintings in Aberdeen. As I dip my face into hot suds, Waterhouse's girls appear, with their bronze coal-scuttles, alabaster-breasted above the squat disgorging beast-fountain below their

bellies. Detached, barely visible, one rears her bin, nipples extruded, as
he evacuates a full desire, is satisfied far under her. Others pout, loll, are
a rustle of puce skirts, a scent of Roman amphitheatres. What less
appropriate image could there be for the swollen money-skin of
Scotland?

67

Waterfalls in Glen Nevis

They emerge out of butcher's trays of kidneys, flecked with black,
erupt over stones Millais painted Ruskin on, plunge through jet funnels,
crossing swords with each other, as if sharpening fish-eaters. The shades
of porphyry sew their flowing thread with an undertone of Napoleonic
hardness, a hint of thrones, tombs, as in old churches. Too catholic for
restrictive practices under wooden bridges, they blaze back, aromatic,
fragrant with weed and ling, in the dour face of the leaning kelpies,
human with anoraks. Above them the brook is red with iron.

68

Tea at the Clachaig Inn, in Glencoe

It is always dark where a massacre has occurred. The mind drapes black
crêpes on the gilded horizon, greys over the honey sunset with a wrack
of storm. Here where what they would call *beetling* crags rattle in the
dry candy-box of the sky, I mention the word *Campbell* in awed half-
tones, expecting revenge to start from the grass, bleating. Only a
photograph of climbers wrecked on a scree, landslides of encumbered
shortcake, disrupt the bar billiards look of the Clachaig Inn, where it all
happened. Boredom will out, like blood. And then a *frisson*, tickling
tendons, with the sign saying 50 sheep massacred in the glen by cars last
year. I remember one on its back in Glen Nevis, wheels no longer
turning in the air.

69

An Abandoned Railway Station at Port Appin

In the cut where the iron lay, a spread of weeds and pebbles contested.
Along the platform, there was only the spray of imaginary greetings:
beside the track, some unidentifiable rusted machinery lay blitzed in
the nettles. I smelt decaying rubber, a store of hay in the engine-shed,
enjoyed views over water towards Castle Stalker, decorated with a trace
of swans. All this, and a clock stopped at five to four, and above it the
date: 10.3.57. That was the end of the line.

70

Oban

It sprawls under a stone coronet, examining the bay, and the height of
the grass on the island. Vigilance of expressed hotels, MacBrayne's
steamers, vie with the Clyde-bound herring-catches, roofed in ice,
leprous under the arc-lights. By the station, men in vermilion rubbers
wade, spit, undress the interstices of what they have come in. Rain only
accentuates the Mackintosh gloss of the Caledonian, the Vickers Vimy
look of the Marine, Saul Steinberg remainders, gothic, French chateau,
Scots baronial. Under lamps dim with strained fervour, an armoured car
is selling fish and chips.

71

Thoughts About Motoring, at Loch Awe

In a rainbow over a castle, the elastic need for morning coffee, some
kind of a break, evaporates. A low bow, dipping its pot of gold in a
small hotel, sinks all memory of a flying hawk, stripped from a
telegraph pole by the 3-litre purr we concoct on highways. Motoring is
all alacrity, aptitude, a matter of hammers rising and falling in top-hats.
One is never short of it. Another day, mile, irreplaceable souvenir is

always being manufactured, fleeces, galleons, carved in shell or reindeer-horn, Iona wave-marble.

72

Inverary: the Town and the Castle, Seat of the Campbells

As in an American primitive, stretched along the loch-line in the distance, it extrudes a complacency of well-managed arrangements. A hundred yards off they massacred some of each other, the kirk is still halved like an apple. There are duke's pews, clothed in russet. Further on, by the bridge with a hole in its eye, writing four simultaneous letters with squat Venus pencils, their famed pad is a blot on the scutcheon, all chlorite-slate and a wash of white windows. One of the brothers Adam ransacked his copy-books to keep it neutral, innovating with gothic: he succeeded. Inside, most of it shrinks back from the central funnel, blaring still with erected muskets, pikes and basket-handled swords. In a corner the duke's book inviting his clansmen and clanswomen to sign is enlarged with J. Murgolo, S. Africa. In nine pages there are no Macdonalds. Outside, an old man with a deer-stalker cycles towards his dinner. Under the stairs, bespattered over elm boards, the slogans of good living invite comparisons. Golden letters announce the world of clayed sugar, Indian arrow-root, cloves and sago. Even isinglass, the explosive ingredient of dumplings, has its drawer.

73

Music on the Car Radio

Usually it was folk. This time, Ravel teased out, squeezed as though through a greased net of static. In front, the rocking caravans inter-locked, became a cortege of irregular *Daimlers*, threading the loch-scene with macabre jettisonings of dead Infantas. I throve on imaginary catastrophes, the massage of condolences on nerve-ends. Ardlui was by in no time.

74

Stirling: the Castle

Black-rearing above a plain of lime-trees and cinder-lorries, it behaves like a block of rooks, as if cawing, top-heavy with remonstrance and affected sumptuous mass. Over bowling greens, it rolls fuchsia; straightens paths with marigolds, encompasses the museum of the Argylls, breathing drums, VCs and corruptible daggers. Whatever is prim or assaulting, it pins down, curtails to its wynd, swivels away behind freshened grit or a portcullis. It has us all beat for ideas, even Robert the Bruce, with his hand over his claymore, eyeing the gas-works for a sight of the English.

75

Stirling

Up early, in the aftermath of that wind of manure, one saw the tartan museum, sacred to the energy of John Cowan, faithful to 1639 and the new Dutch style. Along the king's knot in the valley, that submerged Aztec penal-square of green, boys with hard marine voices were hurdling. Overhead a military helicopter beat the breath out of the territorial air above the spur battery. Somewhere under a slanted vault or headstone, perhaps the confident hoar pyramid near the summit, the king's tutor yawned in history. I saw the wool bonnet of a bearded man from the Youth Hostel tip the steel of his MG with a blood-cockade.

76

The Statue of Bruce at Bannockburn

He was there, Verrochio-proud on a grey plinth, horse draped with caparisons, head in a mail balaclava. Cantering into flung rain behind the drum of the cairn circuit, he rallied the slack flag, a trifle nautical along its masonic staff. Now a riderless horse trots along the fenced hedge. After the black flags, and the crisis, all that was left for the Bruce was a realm, spiders, and text-books. I salute the be-crossed heart-slope of his shield, immortal valentine. Turning to the car, sentimentality is subdued to the still bulk of the castle, royal Stirling.

77

Hamilton

What to be expecting melds with the high-rise immense soot of Motherwell, so many miles of fumed industrial haze, prosperity rampant. And then the blockades of clover-leaf, Bothwell Bridge disappeared under Jensens accelerating for the M46 and Glasgow. After that, a disoriented entry, swearing drivers, wrong lanes, the Scala gone into a Bingo hall, no Roxy, Peter's a chip-shop where Tony's was. Then, walking. It all falling, sliding, back into place. As expected, Kinburn dissolved for a pair of Siamese Tudor twins, a car-park where the gambling men ran from the police. If the brick-works was a brick-works, it lay idle: rusted pulleys at ease above raw red. In May Street the pre-fabs my Uncle Hugh said would last five years had survived twenty. So much unaltered, received into the carnal vigilance of memory.

78

My Aunt

I see her in her own house, one I have never visited. The same grey suite is as clean as in 1921, the boatmen in Largs Bay still blur in their water-colour. Behind glass the views of Lanarkshire are no more foxed than my own anthologies, a few hand-written Christmas cards. Through a smile echoing her daughter's, she opens the door, astonished, cautious. Not until serving tea has she surmounted the profound ha-ha we confront her with. Then it all slurs into a domino sequence of dots and deaths, double sixes and expected weddings. Whatever kin could be, or will try to, establishes symmetry here, is entailed with all attemptings of mutual concern. I leave in my own dream, as she stays in hers, two ships confronting on the hard waters, departing in separate darkness, hers perhaps no nearer than mine.

79

Dumfries

To be all red, more even than Aberdeen is grey, or Bath golden-soot, is certainly original, probably unique. Where Burns died, a costive air attracts whispers, causes a deliberate avoidance of the bed, the names gashed by his diamond in the study-window. Imagine a poet so desperate he would hack his own name into glass, rather than not write. One learns a terrible lesson, rain wearing rocks away in the brain, as wind red sandstone. In St. Michael's yard, the pastel Burns mausoleum upstages the calm gingerbread of those levelled avenues, reared pediments, pinnacles above citizens who died of cholera. Even as I write this in the room Charles Edward Stewart held his council in, some breath of dread, red sky in the night of trouble, returns and mists. He was the same age as me when he died. I write *Burns*, I mean my father.

80

Thoughts at the Border

Perhaps at the edges, in the margins, one feels more vulnerable. Mysterious enigmas, vaulting cataclysms, emerge cat-wise from under stones. Even in the fed, replete security of having written, one senses a river flowing South, away from the blood-source. Perhaps there, in elaborate London, Scotland will re-think itself. Tonight it pricks, howls, is a lubricant and a spindle, weaving and toiling. I card it in words, and hope.

3

THE ANALYSIS OF CARING

TO A MOUSE

after Burns

Don't be so scared,
mouse. I'm not going
to chop your nose off

with a plough-cleaner,
or harry you into
the hay-stubble.

It's too hot, for
one thing, and I like
your glossy fur. So

don't sit shivering there,
jumpy to be off. After all,
we're fellow-creatures, both

sod-haters, ill-met
on the way to the grave. Don't
treat me like the boss

with that toffee-nosed
hoity-toity look. I'm
as bad as you, mouse.

I put my beak in the till, too,
and rake the wheat out,
metaphorically speaking.

Anyway, what's an ear
between friends? We all
have to creep by

with what we can shave off, and
I wouldn't be-grudge
a splinter or two to you.

Poor chap! Your den's
none too sound either
where out giant's wheels hit it.

What with the winter, and wind,
coming, you're in
for a chill time. And no

sleepy shoots to be plaiting
another little bungalow
out of. Alas,

you saw these grim seasons
lagging in, and fancied
a soft nest to

whistle through them. Then,
ker-phlumpth! in
comes our divvy blade, and blasts you

to a bare monkish
mouse, exposed
to the cold. What

hours of careful munching
that mound of oak-leaves
and grain must have cost you!

I'll bet you were worn out
when you'd finished it. And now
you're evicted

into the drivelling rain
and the frosty
morning, without a character!

Well, mouse, you're not alone
in missing out
on getting the gravy. All I

can say is both
your kind and mine
often slave

for no seeds, land up in
a cul-de-sac
after taking all the right turnings.

Yes, it's rough being
human, even worse
than mouse-ish. You're

stuck with a sour dish-ful
now only. For me
there's the gallows-future

up there coming, and
behind
all the missed chances, mouse.

81

Watching a Television Programme About Shetland

Up there, as far off as Prague or Genoa, they pay more for coffee, bread,
even beans than we do. They tell me the islands demand their own
government, have a plan to raise the blue flag of an independent nation.
When the nearest rail-head is Bergen, who can blame them? I see their
blowing piper from Stirling, invigorating the trippers at the jetty with a
fluff of strathspeys. A fluent man with spectacles persuades me across
the bank of lines they need a new deal. I feel them evaporate from my
book, elect themselves out of Scotland.

82

Reading a Friend's Book on Scotland

Dipping through his thoughts, now twenty one years old, I see the
gloss in the photographs, their glide one over the other towards the
endpapers. Only one, Aberdeen with '45 Austins and men with trouser
turn-ups, reminds the years they have gone. I see him eight of them
later, shrill vowels lifting like sparrow-hawks, boys with their loud shots
at verses gathered in the sleeves of his generosity. To recede into the
margins, accept a moment for renewal, is that so unimportant? I turn
his pages closely, ashamed of a calculating boredom, tears yawned into
the corners of eyes. Perhaps there will be a revelation, a step towards
the second stage of one's own attempt. It remains a courtesy to think so.

83

Remembering an Illness as a Child

I remember my Scots doctor who died of heart disease, the medicine
whose name I can't bring back he used to prescribe for rheumatic fever.
In those days they killed the fever with aspirins, left your heart weak.
So many days lying doing nothing in the white ward sprung with

flowers. A Czech doctor told me I couldn't play games for a while. It was six years. One day the Prince would come in the re-born arteries, the legs run again. Meanwhile, there was writing imaginary novels, the foxglove fit of literature to the growing mind.

84

Thinking about the Book

So where is there going to be a way through, back, to some recalled fullness? I seem to be milking Scotland for a golden pebble drowned in the churn. Somewhere in friends, poets, doctors, there is real knowing, a deeper anchor-grip, as in mud at Crail. I keep at it, mending nets, invisibly creeping on, sloth-snake on the trail of complete success, impartial failure. As with all books, it must end. Yes, but where?

85

More Thinking About the Book

At the end of the fourth week, the brain ogles its own disaster-areas. Aware of word-counting, a certain unspecific mirror-gazing, one relapses into mulled recollections. In hurrying, brushing over an irrelevant 707, living through September, imagination becomes a technique. I lie as if with spectacles off, cuddling for slinky trout in a guess-area.

86

Remembering a Presbyterian Church

To be scratching a Highlander and finding a catholic! Ripped out of the loose passing plates, either dice of bread, or pillared envelopes of enclosed offerings, the past lifts rattling over the lids of bowed hats, polished heads over hassocks. I hear the minister's Irish vowels grapple and blur. Each couple leaves in a grey lean of edged smiles, wiping their feet towards an afternoon of snail-baiting. A Sheffield rain still pelts through the scruff of exile, enshrining a ruck of Celts in the mosaic of belonging.

87

An Old Scottish Poet

It would be the humour that did it, seeing *the poets* rise and fall. Altering fork and knife across the reflective mahogany of 1963, he turns a mountain-face of apparently coarse reserved mica towards the bristle of whatever pigs eat and are eaten by, courteous to their forked hooves. Whenever he smiles, that white hood lifts in the crown of Slioch, I see him come down alone, as Moses, bearing no tablets except the granular wisdom of his own poems. And the clean silver face he mourned for, more gentle than owls, clears plates to the kitchen. On another day, with an ex-policeman, and a pair of drivers, one Welsh, I hear her flames crackle into crocus. An underground that needs her has telephoned, arrived, shaken her fingers loose for a time from his brittle wrist. Never doubt they will come again, particular as minor insects, more cosmetic than flowers.

88

The Day of My Birth

Whatever was happening that day, it would all have broken in the terminal sides, mere second-place news. In the grate of hopefulness, the crumpled elephant's package of something too far off to leave even the echo of a Hume's sock, strokes – or would have done – the fur of its presence, its nest in the future. I am it, emergent as a cleared field, a corner of a thatched room. Now it is here, the child burned in the page, hospitable to it: on January 19th, at Shotts, to Amelia Morton Mary, a son. I touch his hand, alive still to the necessity of remembering, fruitful with seeds.

89

Reflections on the Far North of the Land-Mass

In the mind's folded edges, perhaps a place soldered on off another country, planet even, it speaks Norwegian at me, bending towards a Scapa Flow of abandoned rust-red hulls. Under a *shield of granite*, as deep as Cornwall's, a submarine wash laps at the king's wine of plundered sailor's bowels. On such a rock the North hip of my country leans into its own sea, a touch foreign, a bit less Frenchified than Edinburgh.

90

Scottish Music

If there were composers, beyond the invasion of Mendelson at Fingal's Cave, belabouring Staffa into the black wax of my 1950s half-forgotten 78, what scale could express the quavers, mixes, electric flows of their strikes at landscape? So much of it is folk-songs, clan-wauling, a matter of what we have elsewhere treated as if it were tripes, I mean the haggis-bleat of the Scots ram, the military five-finger flower of the vacuum-bag. Will someone, a major this perhaps, or a sir that, afflict a concerto, Cage-event, or harmonic scale on it? The constructions of Mies-form, barbaric guitars: why should these be eschewed, the music sail only on two legs? I dream of a Dundee Sibelius, a bleak Mozart shanghaied into the isles, a fundament of Wagnerian early lieder-writers.

91

Glasgow

To be a city reduced to the wars of twin chocolate-shops, re-entering history as the site of *McColls* and *Birrells*. On the Sauchiehall street of a Saturday night evangelism, closed windows of ranged quarter pounds advance before matt Highland cream, arrayed in level mastered bars. In mean light, as alcohol flourishes, dogs absorb pay, *There'll Always Be An England* ignites bus-tops, a sweet-fight is in progress throughout the mind of a child afraid of seeming English, adapting his vowels to the brute needs of the occasion. The confectionery of the elements wins, rain settles into a Hamilton of cobbles, sherry and first-footing.

92

Reading about the Loch Ness Monster

On a new day, filletting the paper for a hint of Scotland, one page offers up news of that monster, the scaled neck of a staunch resolution in the *Standard*. I appear dispirited, not interested, abandoning what it eulogises, dreams of, to the kitchen sink. There it is folded, minimised, accepted for what it would seem to an English choir-boy, a tic-tac man on the tube, office girl with a hair-do. For me, it should suck, whirl, enlarge to a bloat, although inopportune, concern. I leave it there at my peril, losing chances of wades through impenetrable weed, a gaze through glass of aquaria to a deep-sea dungeon.

93

My Burns

Forgetful of who *The Millers* are, or were exactly, I concoct a man with bad eyes, something in the Admiralty, and a presented *Jane's All The World's Aircraft, 1938*. That was the year of the Spitfire, exorbitant under blue, in rexine as this flexible limp Burns they gave me. I remember amusing a child, as it seemed, their daughter, four years or less younger. It all whirls in avenues of bricked semi-detached moments in Broomhill. We raced in the wind, nipped like the tail of Tam O' Shanter's mare, evasive, contained in mirk. The never-complex irradiates questions. I deal them as cards, beleaguered, submissive, donated to a guilt surface of reflections.

94

Thinking About the Book

It must come, the minute of percipient threading, a needle's edge of seen connections. In silted affluence, the persuasive headlands will start to their feet, issuing demands, ransoming practised excellence, a view perhaps of the Cairngorms, an unrecorded permissive Sabbath in Larkhall. As the paragraphs knit to a point, webbing a yard or two of plaid, it will seem, momentarily, an elect few who advance with the whistles, summoning a whole book to marshal itself. The rest will sink, lashed to some fresh mast for a salty kiss.

95

My Grandmother's House

After all that leaking water, drainfalls of attic inpourings, those damp plotched walls, elastic, unplucked, as the limp fingers pick, hold whatever blood requires of them. I am in my dream of arising through tiers of a red spiral to the echoing linoleum hall where an old woman is slithered through black spotted crêpe to her own death-room. Insides of crates mustify textures to new strips of *The Scotsman*, importunate glass fronts of corner cases affront *Chums*. It all comes to a last crumble of slugs and apples. A Ford, the first in Hamilton, revs through the acreage of my grandfather's manor. My cousin lets the gate grate in little brittle stones, a kilted sixteen. I dredge for framed spaniels, feet of oil stags auctioned in Aberdeen.

96

Dundee

I remember the boom, a roll of barrels, roped, waxed, extending across the river between the bridge and the sea, attentive for stukas, garlands against an erasure of any grey warship. They lay, neat echelons of reflective lava, guns cradled in hammocking tarpaulin, men with their dough hats and names on shoulders entering the cuts and advantages of the city. In rain and clipped wind, whores or WRENs with the wide suits of the 1940s, crimped hair and intensive lipstick, swindled them into high vats of exploding swing. I walked my aunt's dog through them, an eight-year-old with a wandering block of barking licorice, elevated on slick heels, alert to the drones of American air-machines oddentified or in silhouette. That was Dundee, where McGonagall was born.

97

My Aunt's Shop in Dundee

There were hair-dryers, women with crossed legs reading, and a sudden
bonus of sweets, packed quarters, their thick paper tops turned over
and in, their qualities un-named. I remember sucking some, still not
initiated in the grease wrappers of ration chocolate, realising the
shrinkage of toffee-sizes in the holocaust of war. Later the whipped
walnuts, books by Frank Richards, even cigarette cards would return.
In the meanwhile, hearing the *Moonlight Sonata*, knowing Uncle Jim
had irisipilis, hearing one of my three cousins discuss the pretty length
of my eyelashes, I grew to be twelve, a boy with protruding teeth, high
cheeks, and the sexy wilting shoulder-droop of a girl. In the Food
Office, elsewhere, another aunt was again at the wheel of her ambulance,
this time with a telephone and a platoon of captive grocers.

98   .

The Traverse Theatre, 1965

Across the stone room, a strip of light edges. Two men throw words in
the smoke, red velvet itches against the fat thighs of about sixty women,
some of them male, before the name *flower children* was invented. I sit
with them, absorbed by the claims of darkness, mote in the sunbeam of
the old city wall. Upstairs, on the other granite spiral, thirty poets are
harnessing crossed legs to the metre of afternoon involvement.

99

Stevenson's Jekyll and Hyde

As, for example, when a man in a top-hat extracts a sachet of grass from
his umbrella — vide Anselm — and stirs a hint of pepper in what he
explains about it to the coruscations of waiting police in the Royal Mile.
Remember he lived in, wrote a book about, Edinburgh. That was the

other half. A respectable doctor walks home to a naked wanton, strips the last leaf from a hesitant jewelled femur, and is Aztec upon his besotted desires. Listen to the voice of the schizophrene. I sing to you in the dark Homeric ship that sails to hell, unloading pairs of skulls, necklaces of bone-thoughts. Believe us. We are all Scots, puritanical, when it comes to the double life of reason and wanting.

100

May Street

Named after the youngest child, the girl of 1903, it survives after the second of two wars, a stone marionette, plastered with kids playing, perambulators and occasional Vauxhalls. To have a double line of Scots limestone, hollowed like Dunoon rock, laid facing a flat ribbon of asphalt, and given your own first word! It would be an honour at that distance, even is at mine, one remove and 66 years away. In an older box of stone, in another country, I remember the blood's medals, words freely given out of the power of the pound and the handshake. I share them now, only a few left, and the money they bring each autumn. The signed papers, Willy's name, remind me always of what it was to be proud, to have a place, to control and rule. The change of times, decline of a family, Socialism, make it all seem far off, unnecessary, even a crime.

101

My Cousin

With my uncle's voice lifting above his grey spats, flat hands resting aboard the arms of his Volkswagen chair, one of the 20s pair we left in Highgate, I see him crook a builder's smile, affluent, at ease, and generous. In his car, perhaps a Jaguar, I can hear him describing how he gave up contracting, kept the brickwords on. An alsatian jumps to his shoulders, ears alert. For the last war, and all that curled hair above his bad stomach, ruined by alcohol, and the child in the road I remember them talking over in whispers, I ask his image pardon. Who is ever as wild as the noose placed over his neck by the family?

102

Another Cousin

On the other side, squat body leaning in the blitz of whatever causes his
drained syntax, opened vowels, I touch the raw place of a boy my
father boxed with. From the grave of a father who drove express trains,
lay with a paper over his shirt-sleeves, a mother in a bed by the wall, he
brings, as he always did, some tortured flowers of intelligence, wierd
humour, a fierce committal of what *my cousin* means. I choke in the
guilt of inadequate caring, embarrassed out of my English reticence to a
lunch at the Zappion. Here he is eating with a fork held in the middle,
blood of my father's line. I put my hand to my forehead, saluting his
desperate thrust out of the lime of May Street.

103

Scots

So many words held incommunicado, under the belt of the phrase-
hoard, waiting their opportunity to attest an ancestry, grope towards
recognition! I take one from the air, *pourie*, writing the shape for the
first time: *pourie*, a jug for milk, a pitcher. Another I put wrong once
in a poem, spelling liff, as she seemed to say it, handing me an orange
segment, a *lith*. In a jostle of fleece and horns, how many more crowd
to the exit of the walled hole I keep them in, fighting for a square in the
sun!

104

Scottish Wildcats

Whether stuffed in cases, or stepping lemon-whiskered in haughty
miniscule fury from the walls of a myth, whirl-tailed, they excite an

62

envious terror. Who could bear to be confronted by one, however
sober, in the porticoes of a late September wood, or an August shining
mountain? The stories tell of postmen wrestled to death, mesmerising
conditions of unexampled violence. I stir one in my dream of a proper
kingdom. It leaps, bold-eyed, and is on my imagined shield.

105

Stags at Bay

In an attic, or musty basement, heaved behind vases, pots of geraniums,
broken trunks, one finds them printed, shown, disguised as ornament.
They creep out of obscure black frames, raised in bronze, assured pride
of place in the Victorian parlour of everybody's aunt's Bloomsbury.
Condemning England to an under-secretaryship in a Scots gallery of
emotional hierarchy, they stand, fusty with dust, and still unburned.
I touch the horns of one, stroke the steel-engraved feet with a paltry
hand. Here was the confidence of a founded security. I salute it.

106

Scones

As, for example, potato, treacle, drop. At tea-time, intervening between
the tea-bread and the plain cookies, they erect barriers, construct the
assured bourgeois tier-world of a slight sweetness, a punctuation of
currants. The mouth waters to remember them. Handed round hot
from the oven, scalding from the griddle, man-shaped, sour-milk innards
allowing a sense of economy, they betray forethought. I chew one,
Scots madeleine from the lint and purple world of Kinburn.

107

Thinking About the Book

Beginning again, as after a short illness of the inspiration, I feel the
country edge away, rubber-edged from some tar and salt-fish quay of
the under-mind. Slow bells toll, engines whirr in fog. A man with a rope
hat stirs at the rail, throws a pipe in the hissing wake as it goes. I watch,
am indulgent to my own lassitude, not moving, reduced to a white shell
on the sand. Wind blows in it, water flows through, retires. I come back
to the hard evening heat of electric fires, television. Words grow, like
flowers. It needs care.

108

First Footing

I remember those dark imaginary men with their whisky bottles, trudging
the dour streets all night on their way to the end of the year. One is an
undertaker, one a car salesman. One comes under the lintel carrying
mice in a hat-box, one laughs like a drain, hawking rice. They are always
surreal, never seen except in a Scotch-haze, drinking their truth in hot
toddy. Beside the calf poets, brass coal scuttle with *Chums* in it, I squat
amazed, small ancient foreigner to their eyes.

109

Lowlanders

If it were so, though, they were as he says *Buddhist*, what would it
mean? Well, I have doubts of it, even retreating through his letter,
fending off the absurd epithets, boring to such delicacies of language as
in his poems. In real terms, these fantasies, erected at speed, forgotten
so quick, spoil and threaten. Nevertheless, they bemuse, threading a
lace screen, an escutcheon of some appropriate *wild* personality. It
seems a Scots concern, to be thought a bizarre one, a mystifier of the

ordinary. Without it, one lapses, no doubt, towards the dogged stillness of the well-educated cheese-cake mass.

110

Discussing a Proposed Opera with a Young Composer

Spearing a roast sausage with a stick, admiring the elegant velvet he leans in, I skate through some possible halls for us, apt avenues to the needs of a quaint oratorio. We dispute mildly over costumes, glide into a fostered examination of the puritanical few. It seems, at this distance, in erotic Chelsea, almost possible they would celebrate mass in St. Giles, at any rate for a piece of theatre. If not that, then on the slopes of King Arthur's seat, or in some cathedral near Leith, amidst bells, gongs and incense, clapped sounds and jerked words are to mingle. Clashing glasses, an Irish composer allies with a Scots expatriate poet.

111

An Anthology of Scottish Verse

Under the navy and gold mausoleum of the covers, a few hundred pages crowd the dead wealth of a national aberrant ranging: out of sync with the South language, and no more intelligible than Gawain, the tight wry stanzas pout with gross words. I choke through miles of a kind of verse-thicket, abused by the cold whim of selectors. Towards Scott, at last, freed, one runs with naked joy. Bathing in the vapid brine of his pibroch, I note the para-rhyme, invented before Owen, as always perhaps with such, fruit of a careless productivity. Disturbed slightly, by the sight of the two Thomsons, one advances on Macdiarmid: there remains only the blank wall of whatever a decent reticence can imagine from *since 1940*.

112

Reflecting on One's Financial Resources

This constant re-calculating, affairs of powder-blue riffled stubs, numbered P.O. books at week-ends, amazed study of enormous Unit Trust propagandas, is all that so original? The blood leaks into money, rattling coins, a bank-vault of contained resources, castle-firm, where securities, known savings, mix, rise and breed. The mind hums, at ease, delivered over to the engines of a smoothly crossing Transatlantic liner. Life is again a matter of sheet sea, no clouds, bands on the deck under the fresh 1920s stars, and a raffish black-moustached gigolo, in the poster-style, arranging housey-housey. In all Scots bowels a lust for the *safe* burgeons: a kind of strongbox with no combination except the abstract philosophy of a Kantian pure imperative. *One ought to save.* The arts of the frugal conspire towards cheese-paring.

113

An Article about Airports in The Times

In what they would call a *turnover* piece, columned in neat grey, as in dark suiting, a man fillets the place's needs to a big central flying-stop. On his clear map, excluding all but the huge near cities, it commands respect, makes obvious sense. I dream of the dropping wings, fleet shadows above the droning pit-wheels, gliding like soft mouths towards the golden eggs in the goose's belly. Rich men with shillings, welded brief-cases, Holland cigars, drape their broad serge in the back of faster taxis. A new firm commands the open motorways, those hubbed spider-webs from the field's anchor. I sense my foreign, exiled gorge rising, a Conservative deeply useless reaction-syndrome.

114

The Topography of Scotland

In the first place, it was a country of water, as punctuated as Finland, almost, by the static inland quartz of a lake-system. Now to the upper left it is still moulded by it, held prisoner to the needs of tumbling hills, forests gathering like plaid towards the brooch in the glen, the steeled loch with its fairies. Where else do you find such icy drenches, recalling the lost empires and zones of liquidity? Colanders with rain nailed through, those were the shires before the clans came.

115

A Scottish Poet

I see him as white hair blazing above a glare and a kilt. As we offer sherry, he asks for whisky, is a dour slab of granite to our Southern manners, used to the easy shifts and promises of less edgy nationals. Much later, the hair blazing higher, I hear the shrill blade of his voice rise and chop in the dry air of the Traverse, massacring hecklers across a dispute on folk-song. Years fall away like broken leaves as he shouts, the naked viking in him strides out rigid to battle, shaking a two-sided sword. To be so unfair, so grand with it, so prejudiced and magnificent! Those years of educating scoundrels, trouncing vagabonds, emerge as the ground-base of his haggard poise, wavering plain-as-prose verse.

116

Exile

In the middle of *La Clemenza di Tito*, lights out, sound razing the roof-beams to an ash of clapping hands, the incision within the artery of a flowing numbed regretfulness took place. As in a mirror, the long-dress of a donned insignia trembles, blurring towards the margins of another role. Nails in my palms, I let the music crash me to a mercy of accepting calm.

117

Scottish Women

Is there a difference between them, some red freckle, indrawn gene
lengthening the mini-kilt to a close knee of confiding dexterity?
Falsetto origins, a history of demonological puissance, moments of
dark stabbing, as, e.g., Mary's, affect the issue: *ladies from hell*, the
soubriquet of the other half, still attaches, weightily, to their own
propriety. I watch an imagined roomful of them, hats firm down,
intoning choral magnificence beneath the pennon of Sir Malcolm, a
wartime knuckling to the needs of the three-legged world.

118

My Father's Standard 9

That short hump, elephant's back across the rough hills of Cumberland,
articulate energy at a maximum of 63 once, comes back in the swept
hulls of 1970, paraded through crushed monkey-shells at Earl's Court.
I see the brown leather, black scarred paint, the nose of a bonnet raked
against the strip of on-going tar macadam. Motoring as a concept,
holiday as a desire, merge into one or two forgotten journeys, memories
of silent Telegraph poles, glum staring sheep, muffins under silver
domes on the A1. If the *way to Scotland* was a tunnel, here was the
submarine, the dark bullet fired through the last yards of the 1930s,
meshing its harsh gears against a brutal decade of unforgiveable dying.

119

My Cousins

I see a lawn, bright sun, a swing moving, and the young ginger one
admiring a twelve-year-old's lashes, jaunty, flirtatious against the East

Coast light. If there were three sisters, the only other remembered is
there in a photograph, a dark smiler beside the private RAF soldier
in blue. Perhaps the eldest was auburn, too. History in the blood's eye
demands it, errs on the side of a colour sharing. I hear the word *three*,
count the magic in it. It rhymes, off-rhymes, with Dundee.

120

The Anniversary of My Father's Death

At this stage, the whole thing resolves into long fragments. Twenty
eight years remind the carbon to slide, mind reckon with what more
there could be to say, feel, know. Outside, the warm night affords its
protective cover to hedge-hogs, owls, whatever insects remain for
winter; indoors the images move one over the other towards midnight.
I lie on my back, as always, file propped on my knees, attempting some
resolution. The shell falls again, raking the Botanical Gardens with its
final hiss, head-severing toboggan-fall of blasting air. I hear my own
tears in the egg-timer of tomorrow. October is a lonely month.

121

First Sight of An Editor

Above my head in the office, tacked up, his mauve and silver strip of
concrete poetry glitters, reminiscent of obscure blackcurrant and
licorice wrappers from 1939. I see him as first in the barrel-vault of a
cellar in the Grassmarket, well after twelve, smoke swirling in the tense
glimmer of dancing and rock, women armed on benches, men thick with
liquor and virulence. Through a quarrel, near fight, over a poet's wife, I
see his fair squared head, am feeding him money, know later that white
maintained magazine, greedy for good poems. I wish him well in
Australia, dream of him roughing up the aboriginals.

Scotland and Her Exiles

Perhaps it is what she lacks, aborts, or distances, I mean an assured grace of presence, position, I miss least, have no drive to feel pity for. Here in the margins, brittle fringes, so many breakaway successes entail one's own travail. Karl at *The Listener*, firm-jawed as a rock, with the brain of a lighthouse drilling holes in the ocean, *superMac* with the waistcoat ease of a transparent Southerner, absolving crofts and pot-holes of all blame for some momentary delayings. To be in the English vacuum, demands an arrogance of the bold, arranges chances for an empire of security. Back there, in the small abuse of all greatness, what sour cankers plead against these achieved honours!

123

A Scottish Prime Minister

Prim above half-spectacles, a 14th something, to be caricatured with a cricket bat, applied to for a donation, I see him as the embodiment of modesty in power, a block against the hard Scottish hatred and energy. To have got there by surprise, insouciant amidst heavier contenders with their bells and economies, and then to have stepped lightly aside, providing a small bare field with a place in the sun! Sir Alec, as it is now, I salute you in withdrawal, prevail, if you will, over our inbred tendency to accept oppression, call the best English, be weak and hard done by.

124

Looking Back on the Anniversary of My Father's Death

Three days after it, in a sense of dust settling, rubble descended into the elements, I plead with incompetence for a break of the block. Now, surely, at the nodal point, remembering, penetrating, as a man drives his own head against a girl's desire, there is time, chance, an opening to the lost vaults and treasures of understanding. Deep in these, I emerge as a child in a wolf suit, dreaming a bedroom full of trees, tremendous at the brink of acknowledged supremacies. The treasure is anchored, sunk in the sand-shift of the pit-bottom, the sly gleam of a broken Venus pencil. I recall 2Bs, their soft rub, the hard thin etching of 4Hs, worlds of octagonal cylinders, bright blue and white-ringed, swords and poniards of a man's trade on the boards. I mine my own way out, evasive again, still dodging.

125

My Mother

So trying again, splat back into the water, a belly-flop along the chlorinated light blue of a crawl to the womb, I am blinded with chemicals, tears, weakness of eye-sight, reverting to a reach after mother-love in the claustrophobia of a baths in Clarkehouse Road, where he died. I see her alert, arms akimbo over the ruins of a once benevolent garden, beleaguered by the foremost colonels of pain, terror and the blood-shot future. I feel the hard bones of her shoulders, brave thinned frame, yellow with the parchment trailer of a visa to what tomorrow will be. Somewhere, still, there are uses for such a high stance of glitter, vital electrics of cloche hats, 1920s glamour and a long modest grip on money.

126

A Scottish Educationist

Hearing him speak, mouth turned down at the corners, old neck loose in a check shirt, I recall others, dry precise men with a hood over their word-hoards, explicit and careful as women selling apples. Are all the old so, or is Scotland more fruitful with them, wizened acres of wry trees on the slopes of the 80s, tottering away like bark frying towards a tinder shop of last Christmases? I imagine it may be captivating, contrived, though, to think so.

127

A Prospective Secretary

Interviewing her, watching the squared open-air jaw swing towards the
window, black ribbon at her neck, accomplished vowels abusing
Glasgow, how do I account for the classed violences, extraneous trip-
wires in the no-man's land of her birth-place. Thrown words, sparring
elegances, a taste for the mixtures of plain and coloured, volley against
each other, displaying the aristocracy in a tipped nose, hint of the cruel
ascendancy in the drive of pupils. She smiles out, spare in a long green
something, wash-silk black over it. I muse on the tragedy of divisions —
burning over the essence, bark against sap.

128

Examining My Hand

As in Hume's sock each molecule is renewed each seven years. I pore on
a Sahara of hairy pink, aviator in the gold frames of my portable
gondolas, those lensed saucers of a rubbed spick transparency. The fine
grooves under the fingertips glisten, seem to circle, as I turn it over by
the wrist, palm up, as towards an astrologer. In these scarred lines, head,
life and heart, the inexorable past resides, permits only its own reliances.
As rivers through limestone, granite, they rip their blood track, score a
net of tensed possibilities. It is all Scotland is, a landscape of fissures,
excrescences, as gnomic as old stone.

129

The Museum of Childhood, Edinburgh

Through several floors, talking, I escort two poets in the dream house
of selective childhoods, one my own age, picking the same Coronation
mug, off-gold tin of 1937 chocolate, stock of water-pistols, potato-guns.
We remember the free one in the second *Beano*. The other, quiet,

fifteen years off, is still thinking. Alert to the post-war plastics of
Action Man, even *Eagle* is too old for him. We conjecture, stalking a
common origin in the detritus of toy-cupboards.

130

Newcastle

Again near to the border, idling along curved Victorian facades in the
muddy Scimitar, I advance with ears cocked towards the map's edges.
As always, arrived in the North, one senses the far ripples of the
Prince's stone, a kind of Jacobite rebellious cantankerousness. I feel a
sneer stretch my lips, watching the coarse Southern look of the students
washing vans, collecting for their Rag. An absence of haggis afflicts the
menus of the *Royal Station Hotel*, hints of a Cumberland vandalism
throw the confectionery wall-paper of the stair-well. I steer up it, as
drunk as a Highlander on the raw bootleg of being away from home.

131

A Northumberland Poet

He speaks out of the lost cataracts of his gentle pupils, turning a double
Bell's in his knotted fist, remembering Persia, how it was in Malta. Calm
behind scooped lenses he takes out to clean at midnight, he apportions
boundaries, delimits his new Northumbria between familiar rivers.
Embassies sue with the Dale lords, the Yorkshire terriers, armies pluck
the fringes off an imaginary Lowland republic, ruled still by that wild
spirit, Hugh the Red. I see them together, crouched naked over their
sheepskin battlefield, horns on their heads, beringed fingers gripping
the two last broadswords North of the Mersey. It becomes laughable,
too monstrous, yet taut with the pities, glory and grim candour of a
fierce nostalgic wanting. Perhaps the border wars will really begin in the
minds of poets.

132

Sheffield, Remembering the LDV

Near where my father died again, comfortable with brazil nuts in the
Gaumont, I see the stukas fall hand over bent hand above London,
masked faces of the lost few narrowing again to slit eyes behind their
gun-sites. And a group of suety thick men with pitchforks down tools
outside a pub, run in for a pint, off-duty. I remember them now, as
they were, not flash images on a screen, but real people with jobs and
children, marking areas on the moors with little yellow flags I found
later in the shed at Southbourne Road. I never touch the colour yellow
now without pride. This was the last tartan, a plain severed strip of
linen, fixed on a stick.

133

The Surprise

Here, or perhaps further down near the Toad rock, I remember an
afternoon with my father's platoon, a handful of odd-sorts, doing
unintelligible jobs between the bits of heather, still without uniforms.
I drive the car more slowly, alone amidst red bracken, burned by the
sun as if by nuclear fire, an anonymous blitzed landscape nothing has
changed in thirty years. There so often we parked the Ford, sat amidst
heather eating whatever we had, sandwiches, drinking Tizer, waiting for
the war to come. I see him kneeling, I think in a fair-isle pullover. I
kneel beside him, a smaller one in the same wool. Unisex. A child in his
father's clothes.

134

In The Bath

Made in Scotland it should say on the soles of my feet. Instead, washing
them in the grey scuff of bath-water, I feel the horned slipperiness of a

dour gripping-tool, adaptive to the smoothness of enamel, roots of trees. As once in the rain-forests, manipulative with tail and toes, so now, nail-twisting, one is fitted to fresh shoes, socks with clocks. On the Scots gravel-slide of a bathroom wall, wet with steam, alive with papered fish, I flatten a clean hand to gain a lever-hold, am emboldened to prise up, and out, the skinned hot body. It is Monday, I dry myself on a warm towel, the several shires lie moored as before North of Carlisle.

135

Thoughts Provoked By A Watch

Considering watch-bands, gilded along a grey face, and the word *Lemania* below a crown, I re-enter the forlorn kingdoms of time past. Locked behind the surface, so many cogs and teeth tick and click, as determined as dentures, free-running only within the shallow dish of the case, confined to a flat inch on the back of my wrist. How much we have to learn, small country that we are, from the in-fighting of Switzerland! I see their deliberate armies mounted on postcards, a redoubt in Apenzollern, dour puritanical riflemen assured enough to stop the Nazis. Not all small nations are impuissant, even in 1970.

136

A Scottish Actress on the Radio

Warm in my fibre-glass cocoon, I hear a coarse raw voice grated through the perspex lattice of the *Motorola*, filed across an underground of laughter, women's voices programmed to acceptable responses. Is this where the Lowlands inevitably lead, out of the 18th century crofts towards the slums of Glasgow? I roll the black knob, sliding her back to the grass and the cormorants, a voice of uncivilised abandon, wretched in poverty of sophistication. Either that, or a glory of ordinary buttoned humour. Whichever it is, I still roll the knob on, enjoy the sleek wheel nosing through wet traffic, another world from hers.

137

Discussing the Book with My Editor

In planning how to discuss it, arrange some accommodation between
the competing participants of requirement and desire, I begin to prepare
a brief for the case against continuing, am indeed some distance into it,
wig askew, persuasive vowels thickening over a second Scotch at *The
George*. It will happen, I see already his serious even face reddened
above the mahogany, that shared reach of rock and turf, the Celtic
fringe as they call it, modulating into a common yard of brass and
wood. As we talk, in the expected near future, I begin to squint through
at the Irish origins beyond our own, the first, even earlier, kings butting
their heads through bracken, ready to cross that strip of water towards
Stranraer.

138

Aberystwyth

Having reached the edge, driving a straight line at right angles to the
grey water, scrawled in a lace mesmerism of grating suction across
pebbles, breakstones, I turn, reverse gears, am in train to hammer home
along the A4 to Rhayader. For a moment though, compelled by the flat
wind up the slate hill towards the North, staring down grappled to the
coarse thorn, I adjust expectation to the promontory of present
material, a winged victory and a graveyard of castle stuff, thrown against
far light out of piled cumulus. In the West, here, a pushed few built,
stood, have preserved, more than we have, the shreds and agony of their
own tongue. To the North, the Celts dwindle, scatter to the rocks, grow
meagre, as I do, embarrassed by this Welsh competing. It needs
intransigence, a lonely shore, to prevail. Even the poverty-stricken
boarding-houses, clapped up with their own kind, serving no foreign ale,
demand a small endowment of touched honour. I grant it, am as
Scottish as a broken lighthouse, draining in my own dead sea, two days
voyage from the estuary of the Clyde.

139

In A Hotel at Aberystwyth

Somehow, over dire sausages and marmalade, it still remains a
possibility, the intended resolving of some locked cadence of memory,
in the clean view of the waves hitting white stone. A pier, corrupting, a
Gothic hotel become a University, three raddled women offering drink
in the stale lounge, these burst images emerge as feather-dusters to brush
the cobwebs off one's own homeland of the mind. I muse on the axe-
head of Wales, hacking a useless swathe in the bulk of the Irish Sea.

140

Writing After Bad News

Even to try, tonight, at the bottom level, or somewhere near it, exudes
the possibility of classifying something, oneself then, as dour, tough
enough for it, for living. So in the mid-wind, hearing the sails bleat,
thunder rumple in the distance, a few others may have stood,
wondering whether the ancestry would tell, or drop them. After all,
it will cure, or lessen. If not, a man tried, anyway, to accept it smiling,
or at least with a little acumen, still writing. That puts a kilt on the
knees trembling.

141

Re-Starting The Book

Here in the keel of the year, returned from a foray so close to the
bucklers of Scotland, I iron out the first sheet for 56 days in the flaying
glow of an Adam-lamp. Words grovel under the carbon, irate with
embittered neglect. It is all Scottish, even the havering, the delay for so
much time, redeemed in a sudden *douche* by the oil-gush of a
conscience-stricken revival. I hear the wireless grumbling in the kitchen,
a ping for supper's meat in the oven, drive another foot through the old

year snow of another perhaps wasted page.

142

A Drink With Friends Near the Border

Facing a gauze fire, in the real heat of something piped, aware of the huge blank screen and the door closed to the library I met him in, I conduct a wary reconaissance over his Scotland. Wife half Scots in the other chair, he retails her broken leg somewhere, I think near Dumfries, praises the good nature of the hospitals. Their surprise at his writing to thank them puzzles him. In the icy violence of the North, one imagines so many undone by the slime on stones, poor foot-holds. He hands me Dean Ramsay, urges a flip through it, I withdraw before their too-sweet sherry, revolving the book in my mind. How many like him bite up in retirement through the crust of the wall-space towards the soft under-belly of the Lowlands!

143

New Year

Knowing the crust of sugar outside on the ground, rough pelt of the cat slung by the radiator, I hear the brilliance of a sleazy decade snicker out on a black screen, watching a poor comedian jam out a song in fake Edinburgh, waiting for Andy Stewart, and perhaps even *The Scottish Soldier*. Yes, it will still bleed water from tired eyes, though, the pumped sentimentality of Nationalism still gushing in the tail of 1969. *Scotland*, always the appropriate word for the year's end, cathedrals of it on the B.B.C., the Hogmanay party with its ancient hair-styles and bandoliers on Thames. With the clock's dire hands inching up midnight, I slide fingers into the throat of resistance, have to grow sick of it.

144

Auld Lang Syne

Now, on the brink of the held hands, *Auld Lang Syne* linked into the
bitter guts of eleven million by the thin light of dished boxes, I begin to
crumble deeper into the slow brine of nostalgia. Lulu's block hair and
fringed skirt as she mouths at the iron penis on a string they hand her,
only ushers in the drill of the pibroch, something little twisting far off
in the bottom of the intestines. I reach gently in, lift it out, shivering,
stroke its wet coat as the rest do, won over, believing still in the faith
shovelled through the blood by a new hand of glory. So 1970 opens
blind eyes like a cat's, blue, and I kiss its head, sure there will be
another chance.

145

First Foot

I touch it, black as coal in its own shoe, left and rough-laced, already
flexed under the tendons pressed at the ankles. Tomorrow, or soon,
standing on it, I shall feel the early yards of 1970 prepare themselves,
white Indian carpet, green stairs, red felt upstairs. Later, there will be
the snow, flags, accelerator and brake, the toes gripping speed over the
M4 or the North Circular. I feel the year quicken, rage forwards towards
where I was born, came from.

146

St. Andrew's Day

In my pigskin diary, pitted, mustard-yellow, I nip the gilt-lined edges
with tough fingers, leafing. feeling, through the few named days,
reaching for his, not knowing who he was, St. Andrew. I remember the
blue-and-white diagonal cross, flag of Scotland, so much less complex,
nautical, than the Union Jack, more geometrical, modern, than the

red-and-yellow royal lion. Is heraldry a kind of foreshadowing of that future snobbish tourism it flounders, sinks, in? I hear the American vowels dredging for ancestry in Princes Street, striking my hand on November 30th, St. Andrew's Day. I salute you, sir.

147

Lecturing in Edinburgh

I remember the Hume Tower, white oblong from the fallen stone of George Square, a block from where I lived, thronged with hail in the onslaught of a late November wind. After an hour in Grant's, lucky with Tennysons in white calf, and a brace of gilt Rossetti's, I hump a soaked parcel through cold smoking darkness towards my lecture. They wait, serious, a sparse few in for a warm seat from the cold, or a sneer at the soft South. I read, joke, work over them, barely easing a muscle or two in the threadbare tense shoulders of their indrawn sensitivity. I pause, massaging my own dead self as it seems, aware again of the years breaking between Shotts and London.

148

My Birth Certificate

I touch the thin strip of paper, feel the rough strokes of the sloping copper-plate, dark blue-black, the stamped areas mauve. This was the 40th birth in 1932 in the district of Calderhead in the County of Lanark. By some freak of chance, the registrar is named Calder, too. At 21 Hill Road, Shotts, at 5:15 a.m., on the 19th of January, 1932. To George MacBeth, described as engineer draughtsman, and Amelia Morton MacBeth, neé Mann, married as they were on April 10th 1929 at Blythswood, Glasgow, a son, George Mann MacBeth. Only the facts grip, the mind hauls off, too deep in it to know where to begin.

149

My Mother's Will

I remember going out to buy the form, up Glossop Road to a
stationer's, on her last morning. The simple typing, complex red seal of
Scotland with its embossed wax thistle, garnish the dead ends, nerves
broken off between two living things, one of the closest then known to
me in the world. Hearing again her breathing, seeing the huge arch of her
body against the screens, I pray for the tears to start, even on this dry
Sunday, so far off, so tortured by other fears. At the end of this year, I
struggle towards the 19th since her death with only four times what she
left me. I remember her last words, to me only, the others gone, and
now the blanketing weight of death has settled, moved her on, pinned
me here in Richmond, married, without sons, writing.

150

One of My Cousins

Now I remember the glamorous one, twenty years my elder, twisted
wry mouth smiling, dark hair and drawl, a sense of the wicked lady
about her. It is early evening somewhere, in a bedroom, perhaps
Sheffield, unknown. I complain of being teased, even tortured, by her.
Eight year old misery slithers into the mind's corners, blurred as a
daguerrotype. Later, how many years, perhaps ten or twelve, I stand in
a neat suit with red stripe in checks, watching her propped white-
shawled in a hospital bed, having or having had her first child. At
Jedburgh they rode to the sheep, waxed rich, grew to another myth,
border farmers, gentlemen's ilk. Then there were rumours of a lorry
carting all her belongings out of his house in the middle of the night,
divorce-tricks. She must be nearly sixty now, someone I see in my
head's eye as a girl, debutante of a cruel feminine capriciousness.

151

Another Cousin

Ex-Ghurka with an empire of washing-machines, her first husband died
too far out and suddenly for a child's memory. I see her pleading with
that wicked sister for me, interceding against a savage playfulness, and
then presiding beside an elegance of prepared foods, domestic-science-
trained in Glasgow. To be able to cook as a professional, amidst so
many active amateurs, and obtain their praising! Perhaps there was tact,
a gloss of secured diplomacy in this, too. She becomes in retrospect a
cabinet of ingenious mediating, a peace-counsellor in the wars of
Hamilton. But most of all I remember her second husband in his blazer,
marrying for the first time aged 38. It seemed so old then, to the boy I
was, my own age.

152

Luing Cattle

They bore towards me out of the *Business Section*, two white in the
middle, one with spread ears, attentive, as if out of proportion, drawn
by Hicks or some other primitive. Must it always be so, the charm of
the Highlands reduced to a kind of toy farming, no-one believing the
beef and milk heart of such lovables? I wish them well, yards of
deserted crofts without roofs or glass re-ordering into a massive clan-
structure of independent glory across the torn moors of my dream.

153

Mackintosh

At the time, standing beside the *Sezession*, under Klimt's owls and
flowers, awed by the pierced metal ball, and the plaques with Athena in
silver for door-handles, I never recalled the blood-tartan of Mackintosh
in the Willow Tea Rooms, no longer there, the crumbs gone rusting with

the stained wavy glass and the puritanical high chairs into the rubble-
heap. Was the Glasgow Art School, that dour stone monolith, the
original seed of so many far-flung erect orders, capitals? I think of the
quirkiness and the hard flair for a sort of French logic, the Scottishness
of Scottish art, so often forgotten, derided. Mackintosh, I salute you·in
retrospect, magnificent bare classic.

154

A Friend In Sheffield

Touching the pale lined blue sheets, a pair of them, and imagining her
on that stick now, skating on poor syntax, I arrive at another estimate.
Across the wall in that strange 30s crescent, it was England. I see her
daughter — who she now says, bringing tears to my eyes, tells her five
children the photograph of me at York was of "someone like my brother
when we were young," — half-grown by the split fence, on the near side
of which I romp with a black spaniel, Smuts. My father, gangster-style,
with a cigarette drooping and a hand over his eyes, does his Bogart face,
a suffering glare against the light or the boredom, waiting for the
shutter to snap. In Sheffield, even there, we had a sense of the border,
besieged in our own semi-detached.

155

A Boy With Fair Hair

A strange incident. I remember a boy at school once, in the IDG, as we
cleared our limp margarined half slices at a 4.15 tea, saying he'd treat
the Scots like Hitler did the Jews. No sense of a joke, arms folded, fair
hair like Geoffrey Hamm's when we had him there to defend Fascism.
It never came to anything, now it drops sheer through the floor of
recollection, without context or future, only a worn strange pebble on
a shore of power and brutality. I shake it off, uneasy, scarcely casual.

156

Myself as Head Prefect

Swaggering in that yellow hogskin waistcoat, without pockets, washed
with saddle-soap, the only one in the school, I echo through the stone
corridors like a warder, no, the government, admired and feared by the
proletariat of the young and inefficient. We beat them one at a time
across the stripped ping-pong table, inventing a barred slipper, then a
black galoshe, as new weapons of punishment. I broke the record,
fifteen I think it was, all entered black and blue in a lined exercise book.
The new head was in my pocket, or so I thought, vicious nineteen, the
oldest boy in the school, rich in power never to be known again. After
that, where was there to go but down? Fleming, I understand you,
Victor Ludorum in the English palatinate: later, there is only a Bond,
a simulacrum, to invent, suffer, be supplanted by. Such, perhaps, as
poetry. Is it so bitterly Scottish, to need the resolutions of such a paltry
authority, glut oneself on the trappings of eminence?

157

Friends of My Father's

As their card opens, nondescript, a bit religious, not, as I wanted, a stage
coach with a ribbon, I remember a man in plus fours beside a motor-
bike and side-car, and a girl with a cloche hat. Theirs were the free days
of the broken 20s, roaring over the empty roads out of working-class
Glasgow towards the South or the Trossachs, thirty years before the
Hell's Angels blazed in the black sky of California. I see them driving,
goggles, dusted, over their eyes, fists tight on the rubber handle-bars,
women glazed under the low humps of the encased seats to their left.
One is my father, the other him, his alive, perhaps then best, friend. His
child is my God-sister, who said she loved me when I was nine, shy at
five under the gate-leg table, married for sure now and with her own
children. I never see the word Sandyhills without remembering. How
frail a thread this little strip of card is, and yet a life-line to a
commitment nothing, finally, will break, to my father's friends!

158

My Horoscope

Those strange circles and arrows, drafted on card, the arranged
impedimenta of celestial *gouvernaunce* at the hour of a birth! I adjust
expectation to the cusps and houses of a little understood forecast.
Avoid avalanches; go softly at Aberfans. No, it was past. It happened in
1941, when the land-mine exploded at the bottom of the garden,
absolving a fate of earth-fall in the dispersal of grained stone through
brown hair. In a comb's tugs, now, I seem to feel it still, sticking, abrupt
as a precipice of death's near miss. I steer through the rest uneasily,
sensing a whole globe's dirt in the rubbed corners of my eyes, believing
in it, if only a little.

159

Helicopter Survey

Ensconced in a red flock seclusion, I watch decaying rotors tack him
over the dangerous green velvets, deceptive billiard-boards, of the
Highlands and islands. Castles, birds and red sails loop, glaze and
dissolve as a rainbow of ovals and gauzy wing-shapes erupts in
psychedelia. A voice with a Northern lilt solemnizes the usual travelogue
of wan platitudes. The clearances, the 45, and St. Kilda wing to the
bull's eye of a million blood muscles softened up by the pipes and
tartan. Sucking chocolates, refusing a drink, I loll in the creak of leather,
feet out, at ease, as dulled by the soporifics of Television as the rest. We
are all cleared by the butcher Cumberland of the B.B.C., massacred into
evening idleness, as ripe as faded plums for the plucking of sentimental
heart-strings.

160

Planning Another Trip North

Fragmentary thoughts cuddle, gasp, unfocused still, but hopeful. A
morning spent in St. Giles, a bit maybe on the Botanical Gardens, trip
to Glasgow, Saturday night in Sauchiehall Street. I blur in my father's
night-suit, apt for a *mortgage* — the word flew, perched, from the
television — in the old world of the North.

161

My Father's Dressing Gown

After so many years, perhaps forty, the frayed embers still blaze into
warmth of decent Highland wool, late 1920s embroidery of woven
tassels, fringes. All over the huge surface, I observe the stepped Aztec
pyramids of an *art deco* patterning. As with air-ships, flying sleeves in
the 30s wind, it recalls an era of cocktail cabinets, long cigarette holders
in ebony, the tight sheathes of women's dresses, capped hair. Through
all of it, spatted, smoking, at large in the elegance of a youth I no longer
own, my father lolls in the ambition of an aristocratic plenty,
draughtsman of pit-props, mechanic of his own future. Here, on a cane
settee, made before his father's birth, I wear his robe, am within the
literal orbit of his lost being. One day there will be a better poem in
this. I end, begging for it.

4

THE PARADOXES OF GLORY

TO A LOUSE

after Burns

Hey, where are you
off to, bold as brass!
You've no right there

on all that fine
material up on
a lady's head. I do agree

you jaunt along stoutly,
though — and without
much hope of a meal.

No, I'll not mince
my words so cravenly.
You're a blot on the landscape,

and don't deserve my
sympathy, presumptuous
creepie-crawlie. Be off with you

and glut your coarse
appetites on
someone of less quality.

Shoo! get away
to some meths-drinker's
greasy poll. You can

loll and clamber there
with a whole continent
of obscure animal

life. What you need is
a shaggy jungle
to hunt through.

93

Stop, now. Where
have you got to?
There you are, under

the buttons and bows, as
firm as a flower
in the soil. No,

you're off again, up
to the Mont Blanc
supremacy of the tossing feather.

My, you really do
face it out, creeping along as
hairy as a goose-berry.

Why, if I had
some Weedol,
I'd soon show you. A

dose of those purple drops
would soon blight
your insolence! Now

if you'd turned up
on an old granny's
mouldy straw-hat, or

perhaps some teenage
scruff's
underpants, I'd

have understood it — but
this brand-new
space-age chick's floater!

Love, don't
flounce your hair
and distangle yourself.

You don't know
how fast the little
runt's creeping up. I

fancy the
neighbours do, though,
to judge from their leering looks.

Well, it would help
a lot, if someone
could hang a glass

down from the sky, and
show the blear
places we

all nurture. It
would spare us
illusions, vanity, too —

even if it did
cut down
church-going!

162

In The Lavatory, Heath Row

Amidst so many squared white tiles, framed in satin chrome — I reach
up to feel its edge — I evacuate England, slide the first minute walls,
pills, between the impressions of the South and the new Edinburgh. A
little unsteady already, maybe, I joust out, flush the system, am a
dapple of mint green soap flushes as I wash before mirrors. Here in the
shallow glass, that entangled furtive Scot's-face glowers back,
attempting its fling, its birth-notes. In a swaying in-between state,
mesmeric, I tilt along airport entrance-ducts to my *Vanguard*. So many
crowding fellow-travellers abuse my originality, it all blurs into sleepy
giddiness.

163

On The Tarmac

Before take-off, adjusting a seat-belt with the usual non-comprehension,
I squint back through the plexiglass egg-hole at the red wing, aluminium
engines, blue twilight. Air holes in through nipples racked in the roof
beside lights. There is a kindle of excitement, a sense of spies and
controllers gathering to their own shortly to be detonated *fauteuils*.
The John Buchan touch is on the arm of my resolution, I stretch back
to a 1920s of yellow jackets, attics of arrested Hodder & Stoughton. As
the wheels turn, the buildings are drawn back, like teeth, on a slide of
prepared moving rubber, the mad dentists come at me with their
scalpels.

164

Flying Above Clouds

Suddenly, to be lifted over slate-grey fluffy fur of some enormous blue
Persian, as tiny as a flea leaping, without shadow, bathed in end light, as

if catching the last of the day after a sojourn in something's stomach! I
feel as though minutely privileged, and yet out of season, not sure yet
of the proper solidity of this new mode, flying. I eye the blood-rim of
the West's eye with affection, as though recognising an earth-friend in
the twilight of a new world. It is all green, dissolving, sinister and yet
lovely, as the silver tube with its poisons and wayfarers drives up farther
to pollute 18,000 feet with us. I scribble in gilt, notice the dread word
Japan on my faux-gold pencil. That was where I was going. Alas, that
there was no money. I imagine yellow faces above the haggis they fail
to serve on the sandwich trays, swish of geishas under the lascivious
ironed smoothnesses of each hostess. Farewell, islands of the reluctant
Pacific! Hail for a wintry Friday, land of my birth! I hear the captain's
voice crackling out: *soon we shall be over Manchester.*

165

Driving Up In The Alpine

It made 400 miles in 8½ hours, average 50, around 30 minutes for
petrol stops. Now, with the motorway, it could be bettered, saving the
limits. I remember what someone called my *white rat* racing over the
A1, radiator a mess of blood and wings. At the other end, in Princes
Street, hearing (as now) the clocks strike nine, and breathing in the
soot-redolent Edinburgh air amidst the cleaned stone-work, I loved still
the blackness, and the speed of reaching it. That was in summer, for the
Festival. I lean, tonight, in the North British Hotel in the first February
of a new decade, uneasy for the past and the future.

166

Witchcraft

It was Jacobs who said so, you'll have to deal with it, and then it
seemed more remote, less applicable. Even now, at so late a section,
perhaps it is only the magazine, with the devil's head, and the sight of
such a mild-mannered bi-sexual Yorkshireman on Late Night Line-Up
that brings it home. Reading Snyder at 18,000 feet, though, is what set

the carbon running to a note for it — the persistence of it, a sub-culture, through so many centuries, aeons. It flares up as second sight, intuition, evil eye — the mixture of good and bad magic warring for the sweet brain of the Highlands.

167

On Forgetting a Black Tie

Unpacking the two *Samsonite* containers, one square and shallow, one thick, I remember the black (leather) tie's absence. How it seemed too late to turn back for it, this morning. How it seemed possibly the way to begin writing, to do a piece about not having it, the perils of travelling etc. Perhaps, even, about the Scottishness of "putting up" with a kind of inconvenience. Now it becomes rather more the black part one wants to be dealing with, its connotations of soot, and magic. After all, perhaps, one will wear a grey pointed wedding grey tie, one will even, perhaps, manage a sense of how well it goes — at least after the expected excellence of breakfast.

168

Descending, The Forth Bridge

To the left, slanting, as a long orange bow reflected in a well, I remember (sleepy, half-naked at my dressing-table) the cool span of it, from the dropping liner, easing its turbo-props into the down-draught to the airfield. As with London, skeins and crystals, this other capital is a lace of glitter, baubles of misty blue, red flicker, the intense occasional flush of emerald against the clichés of velvet. In the hush of huge powers, furled and sheltering, the tremendous awe of engineering floats up, as in a cathedral of the id. I buckle my canvas belt, am a ready mind for the tarmac and splendour of a sudden fresh Scotland. In my bared skin, sleep-fighting, I feel like a slightly furred Viking, chronicling such responsible mysteries for the folks back home. I slip my pyjama pants off, in the piped heat of the bedroom, am a thing in battle, brave and of high temperature, with a gift of tongues, word-hoarding.

169

Princes Street, At Night

Out through the swing mahogany doors, tripping somehow over invisible steps, as if tipsy with Saturday already, I enter the bleak tunnel of the world's most beautiful high-way, savaged now by the puce day-glare of high arc-lamps. It is all ice-purple, overhead office-lighting, shadow-free in the hard outlines of University girls with scarves in their maxi-coats. Along the kerb, roadsters lie with broken wiper-swathes in the motor-way dust of their wind-screens, dirty beyond the call of duty in the long flog up from the border. I pass a maroon Capri, an MG, a saloon. It feels like a parade, inspecting troops, cavalcades of armoured horses. I hurry towards my pie at the Milk Bar.

170

View From the Window of the North British Hotel

I look out over the glass pediments, dome of the station booking-hall, skimming the hoop of the bridge, halting against the black wedge-line, anvil-shape, of King Arthur's Seat. Red-edged this morning, Shepherd's warning, it affronts the horizon with a reminder of Nature, even here in such a presumptuous bastion of civilisation. I stand behind the stove-heat of the pipes, curtains drawn again, statue in an alcove within the enormous church of the hotel, overlooking buses, people moving to work, or for shopping. As if across a ditch, or a fosse, I wave at The Scotsman, lean towards the cleaned Royal Bank of Scotland on the hill, rest my hand on the brass levers of the double-glazing. It becomes hard to start again.

171

Woolworth's

Despite competition, keen and vicious, it remains the top eye-sore of a
disrupted Princes Street, emerging beside the Register House as a 20s
facade hung on nothing. I trail through arrays of beads, toffees, hunting
for a sign of the 3d and 6d magic of a pre-war Saturday spree. An open
steel ring, 4/-, a green marble bracelet considered at 7/6. So much trash
for so small a return in image.

172

Victorian Ice-Cream Dishes

I buy them at 10/- each, a half dozen heavy glass containers. They look
blotched, heavy as hotel-ware, oddly shallow for the expected portions
of such a hey-day. I imagine those heavy foundry owners in the bar of
the Abbotsford, at ease after their grilled salmon, wives toying across
the road with a water-ice in one of these. Abandoned in Great King
Street, amidst the yew Windsors and the wardrobes, puffed by a
talkative blonde, best friend of my secretary, they take on the dour
Glasgow look of an old set of tram cars. I caress them affectionately in
their *frou-frou* tissue, as if through underthings of the naughty 80s.

173

Washing My Hair

I tip this incredible dizzy block that exudes words, like a pepper-pot.
Soapy, inverted, with a scream in one eye from the lanolised *Number
Seven*, I towel in panic, dip again, become a bedraggled rat-head in need
of a comb. The perfunctory rinse technique, once avoided, now swollen
to a rutual, accurately hoses off the snow-stuff, dispatches me breathless
towards a low chair for drying. I lie towel-waisted, a bit Roman,
sybaritic in the heat. Inside its wet hide, a water-proof doubt goes on

ticking, a little puritanical about such a long pother in Scotland.

174

Breakfast At the North British

Beside a pillar, upright before the menu, in the choosing situation, one opts again for the full grill, stroking open *The Times*, yielding to the hotel-swell of a new day beginning. I down rolls, marmalade, am a furtive stare towards my single fellow-guests, can feel the sleet waves of the railway breaking along my back from the Scott Monument. Out there the morning travellers are beating like tugs or yachts towards the lighthouse of Calton Hill. Lord Nelson's phallic remembrance does its one-finger sign to stir them on. I tackle my toast and bacon with an English vim, feeling an outcast.

175

Golf-Balls

They form a cache in their case, rounded like observatories between putters, one made by the best ever in 1817. There were three (I learn) stages — the top-hat stuffed with feathers one, the gutta percha one, from after 1851, and the modern rubber, canonised in 1901. I remember splitting open a burst one like a hen's egg, astounded by all that impacted elastic, worms within writhing worms of intensive wriggled muscle, crushed for driving. In the attic there used to be two sets of clubs, his and hers. I don't know now who ever had them. The rough canvas feel of the pockets, their flaps, and the lumpy irregular heads of the clubs remind me. My mother and father were golfers.

176

W. Q. Orchardson, the Painter

Not having recognised him before as a countryman, I observe the high forehead, fattish cheeks, drooping Stevenson moustache, and the lean bent frame with a gold scarf at the neck. He occurs again, also rough-sketched in oils, a bit Hals-ish, a swash-buckler if ever there was one. I recall his immaculate chiaroscuro of the 80s, Victorian society drooping into the Freud-gloom of the *fin de siècle*, the screens drawn across windows and petticoats. I see again his hook-nosed old financier below the gold shade, the wife's naked hoop at the window, frustration bent into whale-bone.

177

On Queuing To Get Into A Film

After an hour of it, the big film started, one had that 1940s feeling again, marrow-iced with cold, not caring much one way or the other, weighing the routine gun-fire of *True Grit* against a prepared recoil towards, perhaps, trifle, or brandy. Along the straight street, still that nightmare blue, and with clothed 17-year-old wantons fluttering in every doorway, it began to depreciate into mere waste of time. No words spiralled up from the guts about a Viking resolution, a wintry communion with all that was best in domestic ichor. Only a wet nose, need for warmth, boredom.

178

Scottish National Portrait Gallery

I stride, bright-eyed, in Sir Rowland Anderson's grand sandstone metropolis, that rose park of towered niches blotting the end of Queen Street. Across the road, further down, Raeburn's house has become a bank, or insurance. Here, the dark heroes dim their eyes behind glass.

James Stewart, infant with a black spaniel, glowers already over his nappies. Charles, at what appears about 80, has lost his dandy hair, is a broken nose and a Jew-look. So much alert passion diminished to the telescope-ends of age and innocence! Better, perhaps, to be Mary Queen of Scots, folded into corrugations, becoming pure skull as the eye moves right. I pass the Earl of Mar, John Erskine, with a fine family, three children blind, one shooting his father's hat from a tree where his brother was, now disinherited and slashed from the canvas, popinjay and all. So many descended relics of embittered glamour! More of Scotland rots here than in Glencoe or Prestonpans.

179

The Beheading Machine

Named for some unknown reason *The Maiden*, though made of black wood, not iron, it rears from a waist-high plinth over long-case clocks and the Prince Charles targe, omnipotent, ugly, retired in 1710 after 144 years of muddy slaughter. Two Argylls — an earl and a marquess — lost their heads under that sunk incisive blade, numb now in the scarred block their gracious necks lay on. It erects a destructive right-angle, triangular machine of reform and punishment in the dark historical section of another Museum. The Lord Provost presented it in 1792. It licks its chops for blood still.

180

Catholic Apostolic Church

At the edge of Reid and Sibbald's neat street, forced away by the roundabout and the crouched railings, it lifts, towerless, its granitic rounded corners, offering a gothic wheel to the West and a closed red door with a ring. No services are mentioned on the peeling board. Inside, what atrocities of wax and Latin survive in the biblical darkness! I imagine the black Celtic men, crept up in the rain over the mountains, evasive before the entrenched Protestancy of everywhere else, dipping their speculative fingers in the mixing-bowls of holy water, praying for a

saint's day of applause and plenty. Perhaps here, if it will open, my
opera will have its place.

181

Portraits of The Scottish Prime Ministers

I see Campbell-Bannerman in the robes of the garter, a tight-faced
embarrassed-looking man, perhaps remembering Glencoe. Across the
floor from him, already only a quarter of a century away, that enduring
Labourite Macdonald droops his mutton-chop whiskers. Massacred into
power, each hides the processes of annihilation, blood-thinking, behind
varnish, quiet layers of oil and brush-movements. Only Maxton, ice-eyed
over folded arms, bursts from a wake of trawlers, legless and terrible,
never one of them, still aching for power. I touch my hat on the stairs
to Gladstone, born in Liverpool, still chopping imaginary trees in the
thick wood of frustrated sexual energy. As with Buchan and Stevenson,
even here the magic game has its roots, all stand as if playing, halted in
the glare of pipes and trumpets.

182

Sir James Barrie's Peter Pan

One must have seen it, although now it all blurs into one pantomime,
where a giant on a beanstalk rubs a lamp with his hook. Amidst the
crocodiles, and the air troubled with Wendy, I remember the boy who
never grew old, the *Dorian Gray* myth of the matinée world. Somewhere
under the loam of England, a holed bone preserves (unless he was
burned) the impressive swerve of this bald head, too big at forty, even,
for the fretting body. Against a cream-brown ground, he stands painted
by Sir William Nicholson, as remarkable as Chaplin, insignificant in the
coming knighthood of nonentity.

183

Books in Dundas Street

Clogged with a dust roiled out of the tombs and ecstasies of a clerical
childhood, bargains at a shilling, they mix, tumble and flaunt themselves
in the avarice atmosphere of a late January acquisitiveness. A boy argues
with the old owner before his paraffin stove about partnership, whose
name to be on the door, as I treat with my greed over a pocket Atlas,
poems published by Blackwell. Elsewhere, amazed in *Thin's*, it will be
the same, a Rubaiyat with Eastern mist-images bought for an expensive
song, a set of poets reserved in the mind for a later ordering, pages of
Dryden still uncut after 80 years. I turn past the files of *OZ*, *IT*, reflect
on the quiddities of the Scottish character, that such as these should
hold their position, too, in the democracy of the second-hand.

184

Campbell, The Poet

In water-colour, unlike the others, he lies on a much upholstered
Empire chair, up to his pouting lips in a fur-collared house-robe, as
invalid as they come, warming his feet before the absent fires of
inspiration. He anticipates Wilde or Firbank already, perhaps in the
Byron-aura he has cultivated for his distinguished junior. Anyway, all
bloodless lies the untrodden snow towards his success – and deserved,
too – of a kind. I salute him in Palgrave, remember the piece on Battle
Verse I never wrote, though perhaps will. Even Kipling never forced his
words deeper into our common hymn-tunes.

185

Straight Lines, Sunday

In the devastating sunlight, for the second day running, I track empty
streets towards the bus station, absorbing the 18th century as the

correct minutiae of right angles. The parallels interlace, connect, reveal how much geometry is more normally blurred by the colours, rush, noise of occupation. Even traffic wavers, is less of a manic hooting against the lonely facade-gazing crosser with his eye on a dormer window or an architrave. Adams' Edinburgh is here, as though hot from the drawing-board, still uncut into sections, bread-fresh from the first tins. I almost hear my feet echo as I pass *The George's* car-park.

186

Emptiness, Sunday

I begin February with so much closed, not even the Milk Bar offering a dish of game soup or an Empire biscuit, even the galleries barred until after lunch. The Scottish Sunday unwinkingly stares out of havens of green encaustic tiles, name-plates of fertiliser firms, tattered law-books on The Mound. Outside the Bank of Scotland, a man in a cap bangs to be let in, is allowed to hand a package through to a guard in a sort of yachting cap. Only they and I, surreptitious, watching, and a girl with long hair in a plastic mac, seem to own Sunday.

187

The Golden Griddle

One wall extruded into a red, rope-like Forth Bridge, enriched with tugs and frigates, it hedges bets to its left with a score of torches, handled in gilt. Underneath such miscellanies, customers oppose whims with tele-photo lenses and *The News*. An old man with a dead leg apologises for upsetting my umbrella, as I sip the fragile diamonds of my *Pepsi*. As one, the resinated seat-surfaces creak to the thighs of the visiting French, outmoded locals. Money changes hands with a sense of pressure.

188

Old Calton Burying Ground

Seen from the gardens, or the bridge, it groups well against the spare
bulks of Calton Hill, arranges its pediments, obelisks, as if regalia,
stretches green as a tight skirt across the dead knees in the rocks. Inside,
there is grace and absence, a sense of dispirited sinking, even about
Hume's drum, flowers draped like corn-sheaves under the rotunda.
Surmounted by the leaping finger commemorating the four for
Parliamentary Reform in Scotland, it puts literature in its place,
remaindering art as the craft of incising surfaces. As objects arranged in
light, the city remains itself in miniature here, lit by a white sun,
overlooking the fuse-box of Waverley.

189

Calton Hill

Arriving up ragged stone steps, hand on a lion's mouth for leverage, I
reach the Portuguese cannon, captured in 1624. A shell from this
alignment would just fall to the left of the North British, wreck the
marshalling yards. Further on, from the steps of the Nelson Monument,
the wind slams along railings, glides across roofs over Holyrood. On the
stony slope, children in blue hoods and windcheaters play with a
pretend-baby, image of Sassoferrato, madonna of the rocks, perhaps.
Behind the half-Parthenon, open at the back, the wind eases, as I walk
towards the new observatory, pale green domes over grey granite and
Ionic lowness. The old one is a bastion, lighthouse of late 18th century
Gothic across the hill, lowering and useless. Below it, the Dugald
Stewart rotunda clasps its black urn, stained with the acid remains of
pigeons. Dogs and puddles compete for a share in the bleakness,
astounding precision of casual layout. Here is the greatest architectural
complex in Western Europe, or perhaps the world. It costs nothing.
It never closes. A man could do worse than die here, or make love, open
to the ice and blast of all Southern Scotland.

5

THE DYING FALL

KINBURN LODGE

My grandfather, a fierce, tall man,
Died when I was two years old.
His motor-car, a brown sedan,
Was the first in Hamilton, I was told.
He was a dealer. Once he sold
A good oil setter, four feet square,
To a man in Lanark for a hundred pounds.
When I was a boy I used to see fox-hounds,
Horses, men and cattle hanging there
All the way up the wrought-iron stair
At Kinburn Lodge. My grandmother kept
A handful of rooms, a house on one floor;
When I first went there, on my holidays
From our house in Sheffield, she could manage no more
Running up and down stairs with trays
Nor keep the side garden planted and swept.
I remember slugs as thick as my thumb
Oozing from long weeds over wet gravel
And how in a thunderstorm hail used to drum
On the greenhouse roof like an auctioneer's gavel
And my frail, kind aunt was driven half-mad
By rainwater running down the living-room wall
And a bucket for drips always in the hall.
It seemed, compared with the house we had,
A crumbling ruin, a slum on a hill.
For me it was terrifying, sinister and still,
A place where family quarrels went on,
Where my grandmother died, where I'd nothing to do.
When I look back now I see it new,
An imposing mansion, a dignified brown,
Darkening the whole street with its frown.
I also see it when it was down,
The steps leading up into empty air
And my grandfather standing there,
A fierce, tall ghost with a terrible stare
That shivers each pick-axe. But the steps are bare
Only dust and bricks are lying everywhere.

113

190

A Scottish Artist

In love with astrology, or the idea of it, I see him smiling out of
cushions, his wife bringing tea and good cakes as we devise projects.
In my hands the Beardsley lines clack and shuttle, involving Tennyson
in an orchard of roots and efflorescence. An intense cat stares on an old
woman's lap, a hussar swings a mad sword in *The Charge of The Light
Brigade*. In his caution, designed hours accumulated to produce that
invulnerable exactitude. I call snap to my own Scottish classicism.

191

Racing Drivers

Those flat cylinders, the blunt huge wheels extruded as if on stilts, low
scoop for the cased heads, gloved extended hands in the rod positions
for steering twist, gear shift, incessant eye-hold to the hard straights and
corners — these extract a new aspect, the speed-loving daredevil
encapsulated in quietness of the Jim Clark set. Now in the grave of him
and others, I see Jackie Stewart's long hair, acceptable vowels, night life,
as the only way through to avoid the Lumphanan air, the defeat-wish of
it.

192

A Building Contractor

Named after the first Scottish king, his frail cranes erect their
redoubtable belvederes across the waste lands of wherever money is
building on money. I count the diminished men in orange mining-
helmets, glimpsed from the train, headlong towards Waterloo, as the
Friday rain skates in across mud pools in a vault of soft concrete and
electric drills. I remember my uncle's huge head, his gravel voice, and
the hint of dark cigars never far from his hoarse checks and his vigilant

tipping. There, too, the forgotten standards were up, flown pennants in the wind of fortune, later reduced to the brick-works, and the trips to Ascot.

193

My Uncle

I feel still his crackling pound-notes thrust in my fingers, aggressive almost in the nervous impulse of a need to be loved and powerful. I have it, too, even, as now, imagining it to be so much more subtle. The impish smile, and the room-warming redness out of his alcoholic face, a farmer's, or an aged guerilla leader's, echo and float in the cold remote sea of that high stone house his own men built. It was next door, perhaps is still, to Johnny Walker's. I used, almost, to smell the whisky.

194

A Radio Script About Lady Macbeth

With the Abernethy feel of it, wool-looking paper printed on both sides, a hint of those dark early middle ages wells back, is a presence. The date solidifies at 1130 when the last known issue of Gruoch — Lady Macbeth — fell in battle. There with his 4,000 kinsmen, the line of blood went into the ground. In imagination, I kneel, kiss it, bury money, cut my wrists, piss there, as Hemingway's Colonel did, to remember the place of his wound. Even a scar, a lesion, in the mind, is a mark, a showable plaque of concern, drenched in nothing worse than a minute's writing though it may be.

195

Driving in Anglesey

In the golden morning, at even speed across the flat island, I recall Malta, Arran, Caithness: individual touch of coloured Welsh railings, hexagonal stone towers, a distant rock in the corner of Holyhead. These all denote *island, remoteness, Celtic stronghold*. As the car smooths through the 24 mile curt road to the ferry-town, I erect memories like squares in a cairn. Obscure pointers — echoes of the foghorn at Duncansby Head — re-assemble in the blend of mud, water, causeway wall. I stir them, suspicious of so much detritus near to the British Railway zig-zag on the funnel of the steamer. From her, drunks yaw at midnight towards Ireland. I remember the reverse entry, kings with oblique scavenging claymores on the whale back of their pre-Christian long-ships. The arc of the Highland blood still holds the West sea to the North.

196

At Holyhead

Under the bridge, I view the wreck of a pram, rusted hulk of abandoned primogeniture in the scatter of shells, green slats, a gas-ring. Men by a red boat bob and holler. Through the hoop of stone I see that low obscene ship, humped by the pier and the crude brick of the station, quiet and packing for its dark flit. I almost hear the last note of the hooter, bells grimacing, alert spy-faces grouped by the rail without passports. So many goal-keepers and visa-less children of Israel, thrown here from the bottom of London, entrained without hope or light through three islands towards a fourth! It is all Jacobite, misery-full, dour as the arch of the bloody 45, boiling with froth of blood down two centuries.

197

Reading at Bangor

Crouched over the precise microphone, I begin the slow construction of how to read her poem. The slow vowels grip and steer. I plunge deeper as the quietness spreads, words like pebbles thrown in the pool of the past. They listen, accept the difficult, are behind what re-building of piece-meal nostalgia the mind can reckon on. So much accomplished

117

sincerity to sound sincere! Mother, forgive me.

198

The Wee Neste, At Rye

Beside the car-park, where the sea drowned its prototype, below cliffs, elegances of Tudor, English curvatures, it erects a hazy timbering of remembered Lowland cosiness. I shudder past it, re-opening lesions in a memory of surrendered eaten teas, oatcakes and scones in the rumbling tum of another Easter, mother's boy meandering in Largs or at Gourock. Those were the days before *taste*, that so Southern amalgam, became an extract from the original body's needs of bread and treacle. Today, in the shudder, so much distance enters and squats between the Scots child's belly, and its 1970 successor, cerebrating and fastidious above toast and pattern-books.

199

Another Journey North

I hurry leather, tissued shoes, a zipped box of studs into the plaid-lined case borrowed for it. Military as a mock-clansman in American olive cord, near khaki, with pearl buttons, I become appropriate, vaguely pretentious, Caledonian in expectation. Haggis and cabers wink in the wings of imagination's early leap. It will soon all be jogging in the stage of Easter Sunday.

200

The Doomsday Show In Penguins

To be praised — or accused — for a strong Northern flavour! As if it all came down, again, to a sort of swallowing, a gulp at the stern brew of border Burns, gnaw at Scott, spit a morsel of Linklater or Hogg. I leaf the smooth cheap pages, remembering those black nights in the

118

gangster's eating-room in Soho, flicking the metronome as Harvey and Frances posture their umbrellas. It took a Scottish grittiness, a mean canny rage to keep those lost pennies clinking in the imaginary till of a 1964 fortune. I smile, recalling the Moroccan chucker-out in his glasses, Judo black belt jailed for smuggling gold in Japan.

201

King's Cross

It rears its yellow-brown tower, two-dimensional arched facade against the magnificent near Gothic of St. Pancras, royalty below the hierarchy of religion. Taxis, black as incinerated coal from the Newcastle it feeds and suffers from, go in, go out, extravagantly, with an endless cascade of poured suitcases. I lurch in, lop-sided with mine, veer to the Ticket Office, am another kind of wayfarer, ready for the long tracking-shot of England unrolled towards the border. This is the earth-journey, the mother-return to the dark womb of belonging. I quiver for it.

202

At The Platform

As it nears ten, the hands reaching over the cracked *Lemania* towards zero-hour, I hear a bell, alarm, ringing, watch last-minute groups bustle and surge for the left seats. Fearing for mine, I fill the black laminate coffin-top with papers, exclude possession by a kind of offending aura. So much lack of charity on the day of the Resurrection! I need space, though, am gluttinous for the lebensraum of a safe yard for writing. Otherwise, it will die again, the light flicker back into the wick until tomorrow.

203

Leaving the Station

Moving now, past red iron trolleys, boys waving, white lanterns, I eye the trellis-lace of the empty green drums of gasometers before the tunnel. In it, the train groans, exudes its level noise, glides through to the mess and massage of stationery, brick and girders, backs of houses, woven rail-pattern, the faint stink of coal-smoke. As it evens speed, assumes a touch of the familiar shunting-noise, I begin to grip at the magic of railways, the filmed sweet dream of it, moving in heat and comfort behind glass to whatever destinations are available, traced for it.

204

Peterborough

A pair of turquoise ponds, lakes, below pencil chimneys grated into brick dust, red as mince-meat on the brink, bespeak the inserted first extra stop. Peterborough. Green drums, lights in the sky above a greyhound track, the train swinging, through bridge-iron, over water now, and in past standing blue carriages to the platform. The off-wet fogginess of Victoriana settles, is a puddled look on the stone. Closed buffets, posters, and a signal box like a glass-house, smoking, as if burning plums, or tomatoes, complete a vignette, vague-edged, clear-centred, a shot of another pause in the blast North. How far South the idea of approaching gathers, in an engine!

205

Under A Cloudy Sky

Beyond Doncaster, new concrete or plaster sleepers are all stamped or incised DAW-MAC, and embedded in stones, chips, crumbled pieces. I slide by a train of flat waggons, loaded with orange-rusted iron rails, belted with chains. In the distance, perhaps at Selby in Yorkshire, a cluster of remote Etruscan-waisted cooling-towers assemble on the skyline, predictable symbols, garnished realities. The energy of the base, the origins, is already seeping down as the clock-hands reach for me, for lunch, for the mid-word renewal.

206

Encounter With A Scottish Poet

Before the pierced cans, perhaps a dozen, board with chess-men expanded on the table, he smiles up, expansive, a little drunk, welcoming. I show him his name in the gold book, savage it with him as a mish-mash of odds and sods, outdated rubbish. The train lurches as I write, sympathetic in imitation perhaps. I remember his getting a Lee-Hamilton for me, his face always serious behind the surfaces, prolific, hard-edged and efficient stylist. In separation, together, we thrive North as the carriage approaches Newcastle.

207

Entering Newcastle

As the sun drains in through Victorian iron and skylights, the train draws past squared mail-bags, coated voyagers. I feel the heat through glass, tight in a waistcoat with my jacket off, writing. High-up, as we flexed over the river, between the colossal bridges, one paddling in wood slippers, I knew it again, the sense of it all being laid out as a view, arranged, not there by chance only. As the sun burns motes of dust in glass in the page as shadows, I press the scrunch of the scrapyard by the water back to the mind's bottom, death's image, counter of that other way in, the blaze up the A1. Red and blue cars evade my eye in the rust of prams, machinery, sea detritus. The closeness of the border begins to cramp, grapple, as the carbon reels on over charred fibres. The clock spits out ten to three as the wheels ease, the alarm rings again. As if in a ship, I plunge North.

208

Berwick-Upon-Tweed

The water slipping over and over in levelled steel, layers itself on the sand. A green and a red gasometer, high pills, lift above grim roofs. In the inlet the powder-blue darts of yacht-sails and ahead those lines of bridges, arch upon arch, tiered viaducts as in Roman films. In rain, the train approaches gently, begins to curl slowly above the town, as if entering Scotland with difficulty, up the alimentary canal, or against a blockage, an indigestion of too dour a concept of the sabbath. On waste ground, lorries and a caravan park in desolate bare green. A woman to my left is pouring celebratory coffee from a tartan vacuum flask.

209

Waverley, 7.40 a.m.

At this hour, hearing the PA slug out its slow dirge about relief trains, I choke back egg and coffee, tired, weak, unready. Overhead the green-house between the street and the castle erects its paraphernalia, chalked waggons lie at ease, passengers gather with bags, papers. A man in a peaked cap with a long-headed brush clears whatever there is to clear of Easter Sunday. I wait, low in the foot of Monday, for a new beginning.

210

Another Scottish Poet

In the dressing-room, bald-headed, slouched in a chair, I see him disputing Socialism with a novelist. One leg over the arm, collapsed-looking, his book and the magazine lie penned with directions. On stage, he becomes shorter, more formidable, containing that boiled sense of the bourgeois, pressure-cooker of rage. In the pub, he is talked at by a grey man, listens attentively in his hat and brown herring-bone, disappearing as unknown at last as before.

211

Leaving Edinburgh

Noise of children, rain sprayed as in Apollinaire's calligram across the
window, accelerate the train through soot and tenements away from
the hub of a broch, or a slum, towards tunnels. The red NO SMOKING
sign floats in its glass, dished lights go on and off, cool air circulates.
Through points, past houses in pebble-dash with aerials, below the
cracking slate sky, we heave on, dispensing speed as if from a shaker,
into smoke, trees. The yellow-black zig-zag along the ends of trucks
puzzles. I begin to lose threads.

212

Through Southern Scotland

Suddenly, the sun is through the egg-shell of the morning, yolk up, in
candid honey over ploughed fields, fallen rocks, cloud-scatter near to
the sea. The train drives, claymore-wise, into cut sections of hill beyond
Prestonpans, through a village with a bridge, beside roads. A passed
lorry recedes, a gull wheels, carried back as in sloughed air. Sense of
short breath, ideas reserved, little to say, obstructs the flow, opens up
again the slightly costive urgency to be forceful, to get in.

213

The Incredible String Band

Hearing *Disco Two*, spreadeagled into the leather innocence of 9 o'clock
and chocolate, I retract into the blank columns, bad reviews, of their
Roundhouse farrago, veer to the beautiful paper, cut shapes and all, my
student made about their records. *Fey*, perhaps, is the key word, the
subliminal Scottish element at first so vulnerably absent from it, that

sly tiny music in the wake of oboes and tin drums, with its ecstatic Eastern miniatures and a hint of the 14th century, as if in a Japanese re-writing of Oswald von Falkenstein. So many sea gardens, exotic minds blown, in the scatter eye of the ripped Peninsula we still call Caledonia!

214

Drambuie

With the boar's head and portcullis etc., quartered on a wavy ground, it supports, blunt-shouldered and rufus-capped, the auld myth: *remember the gift of the Prince*. It rings as a coarse enough plug for a sweet, suitably pinching after dinner liquid. I suck the lost gold, relinquished energies of it, feeling my palate shiver to the sound of a pibroch, throat-link with the two centuries gone message, forgotten honours trailed in the slime of Culloden. Tonight the urgency, the magnificence of the beautiful losers, hinges and quickens, breaking through the gate of the brain into that weak stomach, slain vessel, that remembers and sickens.

215

The Penguin Book of Scottish Verse

Covered by that elected skater, easy in the century of his poised ascendancy, the rough-cut inelegance of it affronts, worries. It emerges as the adequate metaphor for us, torn in the schizophrenia of a provincial crowded exclusiveness. It comes down to pity, self-pity, for such a vitiating out-of-dateness. I count my friends, thrown or left out or never even known about, arousing their broken Pegasus to a new caparisoning of Highland grandeur. And then to be by-passed by this persimmon atrocity, false fruit of an ingrown national abrasiveness, as painful as a toenail.

216

Sir John Beazley

Reading his obituary in *The Times*, absorbing the shock of realising he
had still been alive, I remember those darkened mornings in The
Ashmolean, pencil poised before the grainy screen as he tottered with
his long pointer, outlining the precise genius of Scopas. Elsewhere,
along those lines of vases, Germanic as a great excavated Victorian, he
encapsulated the lost wonder of pots, alert, aged, and, as I now learn for
the first time, Scottish. I feel again the distracting ginger of the girl to
my right, admired, skinny, and never known, any more than the same
blood as mine in the slow veins of that ancient classicist, the greatest
scholar of his generation. The mystery of origins ferments in my
memory.

217

Highland Gathering, Richmond

Not knowing why it should come here, so close, I miss even the
symptoms, detritus of it, retired into the Roundhouse before noon
recording poetry. I think of that long girl with the spectacles and the
black hair, who came here with her Dutchman, that old comedian with
the sharp clear voice and the measured verses clotting into his pocket-
book. The blood divides like a pair of calipers, the conceits go out of
reason, meshed for a battle, as a third one, with hair splayed and a 70s
look about his glasses, toys with the rostrum, professional and a touch
irritated. Another Scottish syndrome, to be on the fringes, or hear about
it at second hand, worries at my conscious mind, hang-dog at never,
still, having seen a caber tossed, even in my home town.

218

Gruitshuis, Bruges

In that window alcove, near to the overhanging parapet within the church, seeing a fragment of glass, it began again, sense of the impossible jig-saw of Scotland ultimately solveable. There it was, the tree of good and evil between a furred Eve and Adam, porcupine pair, described in vitreous green as a kind of thistle, tall, Bosch-rigid, as ready for some new *Temptation of St. Anthony*, fit to vomit forth bassoon-mouthed, or bellarmine-arsed, vegetable fiends as in a fantasy of Hogg's, a presbyterian witches' sabbath of cudgelled and expletive demons. I saw it as a talisman, clue, perhaps a surreal found object, as Breton sought them, already anticipated in the sub-conscious need for it.

219

Scotch Whisky Truffles

Alarming a whole segment of Brussels with a flock of tins, their shop velvets its own area of imaginary catch-penny Caledonia, subjecting VAT 69 to the indignity of a powdered cocoa casing. I feed eyes on the squat regimental drums of them, black-thatched, as with a roof of abominable licorice. To be thrown this, in such a meticulous *grand place*, all gilt and soot, stamped as with the hall-mark of unbelievable rectitude, a red tartan!

220

Antwerp

As the orange Mercedes glides, bumps, across much-battered cobbles, I remember Glasgow, near the docks, in about 1947. The same bales, perhaps, of cotton-waste, heaped beside iron bollards, deserted wharves, on a Protestant Sunday. A sort of extinct seediness, obtuse flunkey-style in the huge dismembered *Century*, hint of the auld clang in the

starting turn of a tram. To be a merchant city, on the thin end of a
dirty river, later to be the great sea for your tankers and pleasure-boats!
I mark both up in the zoo's who of a money-spinning grimy
decrepitude.

221

Exile

Always out of England, or travelling, the assemblage of fragments
arrives at a more endurable principle, alerting logic to the possibility of
reconstructing it, what the idea *Scotland* was, or could be. Here it
becomes the divisions piping in mud at Beaumont Hamel, Martinpuisch,
or Mametz Wood, *ladies from hell* in the mind's picture of how Brueghel
might have seen them, skirted horrors with instruments in their faces
instead of lips. I see the VCs falling out of a high cloud over Prussian
U-boat nests, vile with the heavy low moustaches imposed by a German
propaganda.

222

Horta Museum, Brussels

Even here, as in those long glass plates in the suburbs of Ostend,
Mackintosh, our own great oubliette, survives, echoed in the balustrades,
fenestration. Later, become upright lines in the 1920 *Palais Des Beaux
Arts*, Horta decays, too, as they all did, some typically Scottish *malaise*,
fin-de-siècle become fin du globe. I feel pride, as before, though, in the
sense of Europe condemned to *le style ecosse*, as to the precision and
rigidity of a stanza.